Mooney's Tannery
Scrapbook 1881 - 1910

Trevor Blake

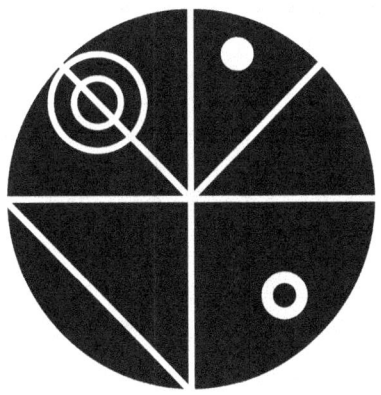

mogtus-sanlux
Columbus, Indiana 2024

Mooney's Tannery Scrapbook 1881 - 1910
(Columbus: mogtus-sanlux, 2024)

Thanks to: Bartholomew County Historical Society.

Blake, Trevor (editor)
[English]
Mooney's Tannery Scrapbook
1. Indiana
2. History
Trevor Blake (b. 1966)

ISBN 978-1-944651-33-6

mogtus-sanlux
Columbus, Indiana
2024

mogtus-sanlux 320

The person or persons who have associated their work with these documents (the "Dedicators") hereby dedicate the entire copyright in the works of authorship identified below (the "Work") to the public domain. Dedicators make this dedication for the benefit of the public at large and to the detriment of the Dedicators' heirs and successors. Dedicators intend this dedication to be an overt act of relinquishment in perpetuity of all present and future rights under copyright law, whether vested or contingent, in the Work. Dedicators understand that such relinquishment of all rights includes the relinquishment of all rights to enforce (by lawsuit or otherwise) those copyrights in the Work. Dedicators recognize that, once placed in the public domain, the Work may be freely reproduced, distributed, transmitted, used, modified, built upon, or otherwise exploited by anyone for any purpose, commercial or non-commercial, and in any way, including by methods that have not yet been invented or conceived.

∼mogtus-sanlux
mogtus-sanlux.one

Introduction

On the West side of the main parking lot in Mill Race Park, in Columbus, Indiana, there is a low-rising wall. This is nearly all that remains of the Mooney Tannery, one of the main employers in the city for generations. The wall is not the only remains, because I think the rows of trees nearby were planted to run parallel to the building. This scrapbook is like that low-rising wall and those rows of trees. Not a history, only a collection of remains. The sort of scrapbook a man might have kept when he saw mention of the tannery in the newspaper.

No one lives in Mill Race Park, but they used to. There used to be a neighborhood called Happy Hollow. It was also called Death Valley, due to the floods and waves of sickness that used to recur there. This scrapbook is not one life, one narrative, to be read from start to finish. But just as you meet each man as one man, read each item of happiness and death in this scrapbook as one story.

I made this scrapbook as part of my self-appointed civic duty to where I live. I would be glad if it inspires you to carry out your civic duty to where you live, in the way that suits you best. "We Help Ourselves."

Trevor Blake
Columbus, Indiana
2024

Mooney's Tannery Scrapbook

A Big Blaze at Montreal Tannery
Boston Globe. May 5, 1881 p. 1
Shortly after midnight fire broke out in the extensive Mooney tanneries near this city. The flames spread with lightning rapidity, and soon had the whole building, which covered about ten acres of ground, in one mass of flame. It being outside the city limits, there was no water available, and the whole of the works, with an immense stock of leather on hand, was entirely destroyed. Alderman Mooney, the proprietor, has been looked on as the tannery king of Canada, having had the almost exclusive command of the market. Two hundred and fifty men will be thrown out of employment, and it will take a long time to rebuild the works. The loss is estimated at $120,000, which is partly covered by insurance in English and Canadian companies.

Late Telegrams
Kansas City Star. May 5, 1881 p. 1
[...] Fires to-day: Albro Oil cloth works, Elizabeth, N, J., loss, $25,000; Mooney's Tannery, Montreal, loss, $100,000.

A Big Blaze in a Montreal Tanners
The Boston Globe. May 5, 1881 p. 1
Shortly after midnight fire broke out in the extensive Mooney tanneries near this city. The flames spread with lightning rapidity, and soon bad the whole building, which covered about ten acres of ground, in one mass of flame. It being outside the city limits, there was no water available, and the whole of the works, with an immense stock of leather on hand, was entirely destroyed. Alderman Mooney, the proprietor, has been looked on as the tannery king of Canada, having had the almost exclusive command of the market. Two hundred and fifty men will be thrown out of employment, and it will take a long time to rebuild the works. The loss is estimated at $120,000, which is partly covered by insurance in English and Canadian companies.

Casualties
Wisconsin State Journal. May 6, 1881 p. 1
The extensive Mooney tannery works at Montreal, covering ten acres, were destroyed by fire Thursday morning. Loss, $120,000.

Condensed Telegram
Wisconsin State Journal. May 6, 1881 p. 1
Ald. Mooney's tannery at Montreal, was totally destroyed by fire Wednesday morning. Loss, $100,000, partly covered by insurance.

Condensed Telegrams
The Fort Wayne Sentinel. May 6, 1881 p. 1
Ald. Mooney's tannery at Montreal, was totally destroyed by fire Wednesday morning. Loss, $100,000, partly covered by insurance.

Crime and Mishap
The Cincinnati Enquirer. May 6, 1881 p. 1
Mooney's Tannery, at lower Lachine, was burned the 4th. Loss $100,000.

Crime and Mishap
The St. Albans Daily Messenger. May 6, 1881 p. 1
Mooney's tannery, at lower Lachine, was burned the 4th. Loss $100,000.

Disasterous Fire in Lachine
The Portland Daily Press. May 6, 1881 p. 2
Mooney's tannery, at Lower Lachine, was burned last night. Loss, $100,000. The flames spread with great rapidity, and soon the whole building was a mass of flame. It being outside the city limits there was no water available. Alderman Mooney has been looked on as the tannery king of Canada, having had the almost exclusive command of the market and employing 250 men. The loss is partly covered by insurance in English and Canadian offices.

Fresh Gleanings
The Philadelphia Inquirer. May 6, 1881 p. 8
Near Montreal Alderman Money's tannery was burned yesterday; loss, $100,000.

In General
Star Tribune. May 6, 1881 p. 1
Alderman Mooney's tannery, four miles from Montreal, the largest one in Canada, was destroyed by fire yesterday.

Late Telegrams
The Kansas City Star. May 5, 1881 p. 1
Fires to-day: [...] Mooney's tannery, Montreal, loss, $100,000.

Latest News by Mail
Lancaster Daily Intelligencer. May 6, 1881 p. 1
[...] Mooney's tannery, at Montreal, was burned yesterday. Loss, $75,000.

Foreign
The South Bend Tribune. May 7, 1881 p. 1
Mooney's tannery, at Montreal, was burned Thursday. Loss, $120,000.

Reported Fires and Insurances of the Week
Weekly Underwriter. May 7, 1881 p. 338
[May] 5, Lachine, Ont, Alderman Mooney's Tannery... [Losses] 75,000 [Insurance] 30,000

Crimes and Casualties
Buffalo Weekly Express. May 12, 1881 p. 4
MONTREAL, May 5. Alderman Mooney's tannery, the largest in Canada, is burned. Loss, $100,000.

Crimes and Casualties
The Portland Daily Press. May 12, 1881 p. 4
Alderman Money's tannery, the largest in Canada, is burned. Loss, $100,000.

Weekly Review
The Phonograph. May 12, 1881 p. 6
The following fires are reported May 4th and 5th: Mooney's tannery 4 miles from Montreal, Canada - Loss, $100,000 [...]

Weekly Review
The Centerville Citizen. May 12, 1881 p. 1
The following fires are reported May 4th and 5th: Mooney's tannery 4 miles from Montreal, Canada - Loss, $100,000 [...]

Louisville
The Cincinnati Enquirer. September 12, 1881 p. 7
Undertaker Box yesterday afternoon performed the last sad rites for the family of Mr. D. H. Meginis, engineer at Conrad, Fable & Mooney's Tannery, by the burial of his twin infant sons. Two weeks ago Mr. Box buried Mrs. Meginis, who died of puerperal fever. Just seven weeks ago, Mr. Meginis, with his wife and his father-in-law and family, arrived in this vicinity, and all located at Jeffersonville; but Mr. Meginis soon obtained employment and moved over here, renting a house at Twelfth and Zane. After the death of his wife, the children were taken to their grandfather's, where they, too, sickened and

died. They were buried in the mother's grave, at the Eastern Cemetery, this city.

Undertaker
The Cincinnati Enquirer. September 12, 1881 p. 7
Undertaker Box yesterday afternoon performed the last sad rites for the family of Mr. D. H. Meginis, engineer at Conrad, Fable & Mooney's Tannery, by the burial of his twin infant sons. Two weeks ago Mr. Box buried Mrs. Meginis, who died of puerperal fever. Just seven weeks ago, Mr. Meginis, with his wife and his father-in-law and family, arrived in this vicinity, and all located at Jeffersonville; but Mr. Meginis soon obtained employment and moved over here, renting a house at Twelfth and Zane. After the death of his wife, the children were taken to their grandfather's, where they, too, sickened and died. They were buried in the mother's grave, at the Eastern Cemetery, this city.

Suburban
The Montreal Star. November 1, 1881 p. 3
Ald. Mooney's tannery at Verdun, which was burned down in the Spring, is being rebuilt, and will be ready to resume business in about a month.

[untitled]
The Dominion Annual Register and Review 1880-1881. Montreal: John Lovell & Son 1882
(5th) Mooney's Tannery, Montreal, is destroyed by fire. Loss about $100.000.

The City
The Republic. January 17, 1882 p. 4
A fire in Cincinnati last night, destroyed one of the buildings of Mr. J. E. Mooney's tannery. The building burned was a mammoth structure, 275 by 400 feet and six-stories high. The buildings, machinery, etc., for carrying on the tanning business were the largest and most extensive in the United States and were completed a short time ago at a cost of $800,000. The loss by the fire last night foots up $175,000 with an insurance of $100,000. The fire originated in the sixth-story, in a room used for drying hair.

The City
The Republic. November 25, 1882 p. 4
Charley Miller, of P. F. Weber's hat store, received the intelligence last evening that there was a position awaiting him in Mooney's large tannery at Cincinnati, and that he was wanted there at once.

Gone At Last!
The Republic. March 3, 1883 p. 4
The old depot has gone at last. At about one o'clock this afternoon alarm was turned in and as the hose reels made for the west end the remark was heard on all sides: "The old freight depot again." The surmise proved to be correct, and this time the fire had a start that from the first baffled all attempts to suppress it. A strong wind was blowing from the west and before water was thrown the entire interior of the roof was ablaze. The department was out

promptly and did good service after the boys got to work. The heat was intense and was next to impossible for the nozzle men to get near enough to reach the body of the fire. The building built entirely of pine besides which the loft was stored with fine pine lumber, 20,000 feet in all, and to this fact is attributed the great heat. For a time it appeared an impossibility to keep the flame from spreading to the adjoining buildings on the east and great fears entertained that Jackson's, Dunlay Gilmore & Coats' shops and lumber yards would go. The large two story frame on the corner, belonging Lawrence Riley, was at one time give up for gone and the contents removed. It was occupied by a barber shop and tenants. [...]

The hose from Mooney's tannery came in good play and did some good service. [...] Col. Rice moved his badly "pied" office in of John Bonham, at the tannery office.

About People
The Republic. May 1, 1883 p. 4
John Bonham, of Columbus, was in the city this morning, en route for Ewing. John is going to buy tanbark for Mooney and Sons, at Columbus - Seymour Business.

About People
The Republic. May 21, 1883 p. 4
John Bonham, the efficient book-keeper of Mr. Mooney's tannery, who has been on the road for several weeks, returned yesterday morning.

[untitled]
The Republic. May 21, 1883 p. 4
A large bill of leather was shipped from Mooney's tannery to Indianapolis to-day.

Columbus Indiana Visited by a Cyclone
Chattanooga Daily Times. October 30, 1883 p. 1
A cyclone struck the set ride of Columbus, Ind., between one and two o'clock this morning, unroofing Mooney & Sons' tannery and Gaff, Gent & Thomas' new four-story mill. The cyclone also knocked the corner off of the railroad depot and partially demolished a saloon. No one was injured.

Disastrous Cyclone
Atlanta Constitution. October 30, 1883 p. 5
A cyclone struck the set ride of Columbus, Ind., between one and two o'clock this morning, unroofing Mooney & Sons' tannery and Gaff, Gent & Thomas' new four-story mill. The cyclone also knocked the corner off of the railroad depot and partially demolished a saloon. No one was injured.

Elemental Fury
Daily Review. October 31, 1883 p. 2

A cyclone struck the west side of Columbus, Ind., between one and two o'clock a. m., unroofing Mooney & Son's tannery and Gaff, Gent & Thomas' new four-story mill; it also knocked the corner off the Jeffersonville, Madison & Indianapolis depot and partially demolished John Ganes' saloon. The total damage was $700. The roof of the mill took down three hundred yards of telegraph wires. No one was injured.

The Cyclone Once More
Bismarck Tribune. October 31, 1883 p. 2

A cyclone struck the west side of Columbus, Ind., between 1 and 2 o'clock this morning, unroofing Mooney & Son's tannery and Gaff, Gent & Thomas' new four-story mill. It also knocked the corner off the depot and partially demolished John Ganes' saloon. The roof of the mill took down 300 yards of telegraph wires. No one was injured.

[untitled]
The Republic. May 1, 1884 p. 4

Mr. J. E. Mooney, of Cincinnati is in the city. He says the American Oak & Leather tannery, lately destroyed by fire, will at once be rebuilt.

City News
The Indianapolis News. October 16, 1884 p. 4

[...] Commissioner Carnaban, of the New Orleans World's Exposition, has obtained promises of displays from the Starch Works, Peave & Co., Mooney's

Tannery, and the GIE Co. Manufacturing company, Columbus, which town he visited yesterday.

[untitled]
The Republic. October 17, 1884 p. 4
Gen'l Carnahan is Indiana commissioner of the New Orleans World's Exposition. While here the other day he obtained promises of displays from the starch works, Reeves & Co., Mooney's tannery and Gaff, Gent & Thomas.

Well Wisher
The Republic. December 20, 1884
A few evenings since you published an article calling the attention of the city authorities to the much sickness and many deaths occurring in the vicinity of the city water works.

As I have been for a number of years resident of that part of the city, I believe I can give some light on what causes the disease which sends so many of our neighbors to speedy graves. Some years ago, when the mill-dam across Flatrock gave way and the water, finding its natural course unobstructed, ceased to flow through the mill race, some talk was made about petitioning the officials, to have it filled in and allow the manufactories along its course to lay a sewer from Mooney's tannery to below the old bridge, where good current could be reached which would carry all the filth far below the city.

Nothing was done, however, and as year after year passed and the filth from two tanneries, the gas works and woolen mill was allowed to flow down and settle at the foot of the knoll and at the very door of a city institution. It was prevented from entering the river by a dam placed across the race at the time of building the water works. The stench arising became almost unbearable and complaint was made to the city authorities, but no notice was taken of it.

A prediction was made a few years ago, by one who is very low at this moment, with a disease caused by the "old race," that if something was not done to prevent further accumulation of the filth that it would cause many deaths and ruin the valuation of property in that part of the city.

If it has been known for several years past that something caused a great deal of sickness in that part of the city, why did not the authorities look into the matter? Have we not a board of health, and was it not their duty to find the cause and have it abolished if possible?

No, year after year, disease and death were allowed to accumulate unnoticed, until finally it arose like an avenging nemesis and made, itself manifest by disease and death.

Blaming none in particular for this state of affairs and hoping that our city officials will cause an investigation into this matter, I sign myself,

WELL WISHER

Casualties
Boscobel Dial. April 21, 1885 p. 4
J. H. Mooney's large tannery at Montreal was burned, the loss reaching $100,000.

Condensed Dispatches
Freeport Daily Bulletin. April 15, 1885 p. 2
J. H. Mooney's large tannery at Montreal was burned, the loss reaching $100,000.

Empire State News
The Buffalo News. April 15, 1885 p. 1
Mooney 's tannery, Toronto, burned, yesterday. Loss $100,000. Several employees escaped by jumping from the second-story windows into snowbanks.

Here and There
Lake Geneva Herald. April 18, 1885 p. 6
J. H. Mooney's large tannery at Montreal was burned Tuesday afternoon, the loss reaching $100,000. Several of the employees escaped by jumping from the windows.

Minor News Items
Belvidere Standard. April 15, 1885 p. 2
J. H. Mooney's large tannery at Montreal was burned Tuesday afternoon, the loss reaching $100,000. Several of the employees escaped by jumping from the windows.

Foreign
Pineville News. April 15, 1885 p. 1
J. H. Mooney's large tannery at Montreal was burned the other afternoon, the loss reaching $100,000. Several of the employees escaped by jumping from the windows.

Foreign
Argos Reflector. April 23, 1885 p. 1
J. H. Mooney's large tannery at Montreal was burned the other afternoon, the loss reaching $100,000. Several of the employees escaped by jumping from the windows.

Casualties
Lake Geneva Herald. April 25, 1885 p. 6
J. H. Mooney's large tannery at Montreal was burned the other afternoon, the loss reaching $100,000.

Foreign
Wessington Springs Herald. May 8, 1885 p. 2
J. H. Mooney's large tannery at Montreal was burned the other afternoon, the loss reaching $100,000. Several of the employees escaped by jumping from the windows.

The "Bavarian" Fisheries
Wessington Springs Herald. June 25, 1885 p. 4
Early last Thursday morning ye editor threw aside the cares of monotonous newspaper business for the time being, and by previous invitation and arrangement, jumped into Mr. Vol. Stillabower's comfortable

phaeton that was in waiting at the door, and driven by that gentleman to his cosy farm home nestled among the hills about eight miles southwest of this city. The morning was just cool enough to be pleasant, and the fresh air inhaled and the new scenery beheld, was an enjoyable treat to us indeed.

The object of our trip and visit was to see and examine the fisheries started by Mr. Stillabower on his premises last fall, and which industry he intends to engage in quite extensively in the future. His place is what is known as the old Mooney tannery farm, and much of it is well adapted to the culture of Carp, or fish, as it has plenty of cool, clear, pure and ever-living springs and the gentle sloping ravines and valleys can be easily converted into fish ponds, almost as natural as nature. We spent the entire day with him and during that time gleaned from him and observed the following facts, etc., concerning this interesting and growing industry:

Five and one half acres of ground, east and almost directly in front of his house, have been converted into ponds (4 of them) and are under water — one pond alone covers 4 acres. In it he placed six thousand German Carp last October, costing him $125, and were bought of John Miller, near Bluff Creek, in this (Johnson) county. He hauled them home in a threshing engine water tank and let them out, water and all, at that time, through the two-inch rubber hose at the end. They are not yet one year old, are fat and plump, and will average eight inches in length; we handled several of them and know whereof we speak. A narrow plank walk has been built out about half way across the big pond, seats erected thereon, and feed troughs attached thereto, about for or five inches under the water from and in which Mr. S., feeds the fish, calling them up by the tooting of a small horn. They swarm about the feeding places by the thousands for their rations at the tooting of the horn, and are so tame that they will eat bread out of your hands — at least they did out of the writer's and nibbled gently at his fingers. This is a beautiful and novel sight indeed and well worth seeing. Mr. S. has two pair of large Mirror Carp — spawners — in a small pond by themselves, which cost him $850. Two of them weigh 15 lbs and the others 13 pounds each, and are 24 and 30 inches in length, respectively. In another pond (larger) adjacent, he has one dozen Scale Carp which cost him $25. He has two varieties of the German Carp, "Mirror" and "Seale." His spawners are doing nicely and the eggs hatching well, and he expects to have nearly one hundred thousand young Carp this fall, which will be offered for sale to those who wish to engage in the Carp or fish culture and stock ponds. Mr. Stillabower is perfectly carried away with his new industry. He is well versed in the business so far, and as he devotes his whole time and attention to it, is bound to succeed; at least everything is in his favor.

About People

The Republic. July 27, 1886 p. 4

Everett Stillinger severed his connection with the office at Mooney's tannery and has accepted a position in the starch works office. Will Mooney takes his place at the tannery.

Greensburg, Ind. March 3, 1888

The Republic. March 6, 1888 p. 4

To the Honorable Mayor and Common Council of the City of Columbus, Ind.:

I, Amos S. Creath, Mayor, hereby certify that the following resolution was adopted by the Common Council of the city of Greensburg, Ind., at its regular meeting on the 2nd day of March, 1888:

Resolved by the Common Council of the city of Greensburg, Ind., that the thanks of our Council be and are hereby tendered to the Hon. Mayor Spencer, Water-works Trustees, Crump, Formehlen and Trotter, members of your City Council, Chief of Fire Department Reeves, Superintendents of the Starch Works, Cerealine Works, Reeves & Co.'s Works, Mooney's Tannery and Electric Light Works, as well as other citizens of the city of Columbus, Ind., for the many courtesies extended to the members of our City Council and citizens on the occasion of our visit to your city on the 29th day of February, 1888.

A. S. CREATH, Mayor.

Found Drowned

The Gazette. April 25, 1888

An inquest was held at Mooney's tannery, Lower Lachine road, yesterday afternoon, on the body of a man named Cusson, a French-Canadian, who was found in the Rivière St. Pierre yesterday morning, while examining, it is supposed, a small dyke constructed of ashes near the tannery. The deceased, who leaves a wife and five children, was watchman at Messrs. Mooney's tannery. The jury returned a verdict of "found drowned."

Found in the Canal

The Montreal Star. April 25, 1888

The body of Napoleon Cusson, night watchman at Mooney's Tannery at St. Henri, was found in the canal yesterday afternoon and an inquest was held which resulted in a verdict of "found drowned." It is supposed that the deceased while on duty Saturday night, was trying to dip some water from the canal with a pail when he slipped and fell in. Search had been made for the body on Sunday afternoon but without result. The deceased leaves a widow and five children.

Out of Gear

The Republic. March 6, 1888

The following special to the *Cincinnati Enquirer* from this city appeared in that paper yesterday and shows that the reporter's brain has slipped an eccentric:

COLUMBUS, IND., July 9. - The campaign was opened here Saturday night by a monster demonstration of the laboring men, who organized a Cleveland and Thurman Club at the Court House. Over 1,100 persons signed the roll. The men are mostly employed at the Cerealine Mills, Reeves' agricultural works, American Starch Works and Mooney's tannery. Hon. Geo. W. Cooper, Democratic candidate for Congress, delivered an able and eloquent speech. It was the largest demonstration ever seen in Southern Indiana.

From the *Herald*'s report of the meeting the following is taken:

A report from the soliciting committee showed a membership of 449, over 400 of which were present. It being purely a club meeting, no one but members were present, except a few who had learned that the Hon. Geo. W. Cooper would address the club, and desiring to hear him, they were permitted to remain.

Great Demonstration at Columbia, Indiana
The Gazette. August 20, 1888
W. R. Myers, Ex-Secretary of State and Democratic candidate for Lieutenant Governor, spoke here tonight to the Hendricks Club, delivering a masterly speech. When it was learned to-day that he would be here an impromptu labor demonstration was got up without announcement, composed of employees of the cerealine mills, starch works, Reeves agricultural, Mooneys' tanners, Moore Tilton Schimner's cooper shops. The procession numbered, actual

count, 763; one hundred young ladies and two hundred boys on horseback, and several brass bands. It was the largest impromptu demonstration ever got up in this place, and paled the Harrison demonstration of yesterday into insignificance. Fred Poe, foreman of the cerealine mills, was a speaker with Myers.

Personal and Society
The Republic. November 8, 1888
Mr. Bert Overstreet will leave to-morrow evening for Decatur, Ala., where he has accepted a position with Mooney's tannery at that place.

Spirited Meeting
The Republic. March 6, 1891 p. 4
[...] A communication was signed by the citizens improvement committee bringing the attention of the council to the inadequate protection against fire at W. W. Mooney tannery, and recommended that steps be taken to remedy this oversight.

This was followed by a statement from W. W. Mooney & Sons, in which they said that the recent fire had demonstrated to them that their fire protection was inadequate, and that their firm had at their own expense put in the main that was at their building, and that if the council would put in the protection asked for they would at once enlarge their works, making it the largest tannery in this country. The recommendation and application was, on motion, received, endorsed by the council and sent to the water-works trustees, with instructions to grant the request. [...]

[untitled]
The Republic. March 9, 1891 p. 4
Councilman Carr thinks the water used by Mooney's tannery comes at too low a figure, while Councilman Mooney thinks that John Carr's liquor is being sold at too great a per cent over goods in other saloons that pay a license. Mooney has two committees and the solid vote of the council, except Carr, to back his position, while Carr stands alone without support. Councilman Carr can be relied upon to look after the interest of one of his backers in the first ward, and that man's name is John Carr.

[untitled]
The Republic. November 6, 1891 p. 4
James Henry, working at Mooney's tannery, was paid to-day $18.21 by Quick & Honey for accidental injuries received several days ago.

Surrounded by the Penn
St. Louis Globe-Democrat. February 17, 1892 p. 5
The Mooney Lateral Railway Company, capital $10,000, has been organized to construct a railway one-half mile in length from Mooney & Sons' tannery to a connection with the Big Four tracks. W. W. Mooney & Sons are the stock-holders, and will build the road at once. This step is made necessary on account of the fact that the Pennsylvania company have Mooneys' tannery surrounded in such a manner as to prevent

the Big Four reaching it. The organization of this company enables the Mooneys to force an outlet and connection with the Big Four system.

Improvement and Mooney's
The Republic. March 9, 1892 p. 4
There are but few in Columbus who know what is really going on in the way of improvements at Mooney's mammoth tannery in this city. In addition to the building of the railroad to their immense works they will spend about $175,000 in enlarging their present large factory. For this purpose a contract was closed for 1,300,000 brick, and contractors Stillinger & Lee have a large force of men at work to-day making excavations for the new buildings. Of this improvement but little if anything has as heretofore reached the public. There are no more careful business men in this or any other State than W. W. Mooney & Son, and the citizens of Columbus will be pleased to learn of this permanent improvement, which not only guarantees the present employment of labor but will give employment to more.

Fire Alarms
The Republic. March 9, 1892 p. 4
The keys have been left at the nearest house to each box. In case of fire, get the key, open the door, pull down the lever and let it go, leaving the door open. The following is the correct location of boxes: [...] 17 Mooney's Tannery[1].

[untitled]
The Republic. July 28, 1892 p. 4
A new mile track, a new furniture factory, the orphans' home, a $10,000 school house, a large addition to Mooney's Tannery, three miles of new street car track, a new United Brethren church and the railroad switches moved from the city is doing real well for Columbus thus far this season.

Little done
The Republic. August 5, 1892 p. 4
The council met in regular session last night, and that was about all. All the councilmen were present except Clark.

Anxious for the good of the city, Councilman Caldwell dropped in long enough to get his name in the "pot" for $2, and then left for Denver.

On motion the clerk was authorized to offer $25 reward for the arrest of parties interfering with electric' light lamps.

---
[1] Editor's Note: Beginning on this date, an identical item appears in *The Republic* almost daily for nearly a decade. See also "Auto Burns While Wrong Number Hits" p. 122 and "Grant Petition of the Firemen" p. 139.

Committee reported favorably on the platted additions of McCormack and Irwin and W. J. Lucas, Clerk, will certify the same to the county auditor.

The report of the committee appointed to give additional fire protection to Mooneys' tannery was read and referred to water-works trustees. [...]

Many Buildings
The Republic. August 6, 1892 p. 4
[...] Several cottage residences in East Columbus and Orinoco are under contract, while considerable work is yet to be done on Mooney's large tannery. [...]

They Are Hustlers
The Republic. August 27, 1892 p. 4
On Monday Contractors Stillinger & Lee will begin to make the excavations for the vats for Mooney's new tannery. About 300,000 yards of dirt will be moved. These contractors will also on Monday next begin the excavation for the extension of Crump's street car line. This firm has given employment to a large number of hands and teams this season, which has been a great benefit to this class of laborers.

From Protected Industries
The Republic. October 13, 1892 p. 4
In the Democratic procession last night were clubs from the Cerealine mills, Mooney's tannery and Reeves & Co.'s works. While no free trade banners were carried, the procession, being Democratic, was no

other than such a one. The men who come from the Cerealine mill and Reeves & Co.'s receive their employment from factories that have the highest protection in any country on earth, being protected by patents. The leather manufactured by W. W. Mooney & Sons is protected to the extent of 10 *per cent. ad valorem*, while hides are admitted free of duty. Not one of a dozen of the men in line last night want to see a change from the present condition of affairs, and as a whole the men in line were at heart, not in sympathy with Democratic principles.

[untitled]
The Republic. December 26, 1892 p. 2
It is well enough to put down good crossings on west Fifth street, as a large number of persons, and especially laborers, are required to go to Mooney's tannery that way, but it will be a great deal colder than it now is before Mr. Schwartzkopf, of the street and alley committee, convinces the public that the location of this walk is such a one as will make a "test."

Fell Fifty Feet
The Republic. February 13, 1893 p. 2
Ed Saladin' Awful Accident May Cause His Death.

Ed Saladin, the 18-year-old son of Jacob Saladin, fell from a scaffold fifty feet high at Mooney's tannery this morning at 8 o'clock and sustained injuries that may prove fatal. He was working at his trade, that of a tinner, and was near the large brick smoke-stack when he in some manner lost his balance and fell. There was no hope for him, he had nothing to catch to, and struck upon the old mortar boxes on the ground below. His right arm was broken above the wrist, the bones protruding through the flesh. His shirts were torn across the back where he struck a board that was setting on edge.

For some time he was unconscious, but when taken to his home on Jackson, between Fifth and Sixth streets, he regained consciousness. He complained of great pain in his back and side, and it is feared that he is seriously injured internally. The family physician, Dr. Rice, was summoned and is at his bedside, but it will require some time to determine the full extent of his injuries. Some time ago young Saladin took out an accident policy of $1,000 in the Northwestern Accident company, of this city.

Personal and Society
The Republic. February 18, 1893 p. 2
Ed Saladin, who fell from the top of the smoke stack at Mooney's tannery some days ago and was seriously injured, has so far recovered as to be able to sit up in his room.

Regular Session
The Republic. March 3, 1893 p. 2
A special committee was appointed to look after the securing of water for Mooney's tannery.

Struck
The Republic. March 23, 1893 p. 3
Just afternoon to-day a hod carrier was employed to work at Mooney's tannery that did not belong to the Union and that refused to become a member, in consequence of which about a dozen hod carriers went on a strike, and this caused the brick masons to quit work. Up to the time the *Republican* went to press the matter was not settled.

[untitled]
The Republic. March 23, 1893 p. 4
Mooney's tannery in closed to-day on account of the funeral of William Mitchell, an esteemed employee who on Tuesday lost his life accidentally while at work.

Personal and Society
The Republic. April 17, 1893 p. 4
George Dalgetta-Kerr, superintendent of machinery at Mooney's tannery, is able to be out again after several days' illness.

[untitled]
The Republic. August 18, 1893 p. 4
The communication of F. T. Crump, regarding the extension of the sewer from Mooney's tannery to Eighth street, was referred to the sewerage committee.

Extend the Sewer

The Republic. August 21, 1893 p. 4
The City Needs It, and It Would Guarantee Sanitariam.

The question of the city extending the sewer from Mooney's tannery north to Eighth street crossing is just now under consideration. This improvement is beyond question greatly needed, both for the health of the city and for the convenience of those who want better sewerage. The sewer from the water works to Mooney's tannery is twenty-four inches in diameter, and is believed to be large enough to accommodate the sewerage demands from the city for some time to come. Just now F. T. Crump is contemplating the erection of a sanitarium on north Washington street for the use of those who desire to take baths in the valuable mineral water which flows from his well there.

This sanitarium must have drainage, and the refuse or waste water from it can not be allowed to enter the river above the water works filter. If the city will extend the sewer from Mooney's tannery to Eighth street, Mr. Crump will continue it to his sanitarium, a distance of two thousand feet or more. This would give to those living in the northern part of the city ample sewerage for resident purposes, and would be general benefit. It is the belief that if Mr. Crump would consent to allow those who might want to tap his sewer to do so, the city could well afford to proceed with the work of extending the sewer.

The sanitarium, if built, will be an advantage that all would appreciate, and many would no doubt be permanently benefited by it. Besides this, it would draw large numbers to this city, who would spend their money here by the way of securing board and any other of the necessaries or luxuries of life. There are none who can better appreciate the benefits of a sanitarium to a city than those who have spent some time at other places. If F. T. Crump should put up a sanitarium here it would be worth to the city as much as if it had secured a manufacturing establishment that employed hundred or more men. At least this is the way some who have carefully watched the growth of Martinsville put it.

The city council should extend the sewer. The city needs it, and by so doing the sanitarium project would go.

Second Fire
The Republic. March 27, 1894 p. 4
The Boys Arrived in Time to Save Several Dwellings — By the Free Use of Water Much Property is Saved at Fifth and Brown Streets.

An alarm of fire was sent in about 10:30 this morning from box 18 and the department was on, the ground in a very short time. Flames were bursting out of Joe Gable's stable in the rear of his residence on the corner of Fifth and Brown streets. A number of men from Mooney's tannery got a stream on from a hydrant in the factory yard, but their line of hose was too short for effective service. The firemen soon had the blaze under control and prevented spread to the residence and adjoining buildings.

The building which was in good repair has been used as a stable but there was no stock in it. Mr. Gable had one end fitted up as a kitchen in which the family cooking and washing was done. He had a fire in the cook stove this morning, but thinks he put it out and had the stove well closed before he left it. There was no one at home when the fire was discovered and Mrs. Gable is out of the city. Mr. Gable estimates his loss at $300 on which there is not one cent of insurance.

The promptness shown by the drivers of the hose reels and hook and ladder truck in getting to the fire is due in great measure to the new harness which makes hitching up the work of few seconds only.

Mooney's tannery fire brigade claims the honor of getting first water on the fire to-day.

Will Adams one of the new fire recruits claims first water also, as he got both overcoat pockets full in less than forty seconds after he arrived on the ground.

The habit of drivers of different kinds of vehicles, when they hear an alarm, make a break at once for the scene of the fire and almost invariably get in the way of the hose reels and hook and ladder truck. Some one is going to get hurt at this kind of work and the city will be expected to foot the bill.

Bad Water
The Republic. August 21, 1894 p. 4

The hydrant water on account of repairs in the filter was last night and today very much affected by the ooze from Mooney's Tannery. When the new filter is put in the water works trustees should open every street plug in the city and thoroughly blow out the mains.

City Officials Meet
The Republic. August 21, 1894 p.

The city board of health and councilmen met the water works trustees at the water works at 2 p. m. pursuant to request of the water works trustees. The object of the meeting was to discuss what should be done with the water from Mooney's tannery, which now flows over the filter into the river.

The trustees suggested the putting in of wooden box sewer 1 x 5 feet, and thus conducting the water to point below the filter. This will come up for action at the coming meeting of the city council.

The trustees are putting in a second filter a distance of some eighty feet. If there is a rise in the river this work will be completed in a few days, when larger and better water supply can be had.

Special Session
The Republic. August 25, 1894 p. 9
The Water Matter Comes Up for Final Action.

The report of Civil Engineer Hege called for at last special meeting of the city council in regard to plans proposed to secure pure water and more of it was the first business of the meeting.

The report was carefully prepared and lengthy. It recommends the putting in of a crib in the center of the river 140 feet long, 10 feet wide and sinking it about six feet in the sand in the bed of the river below the railroad bridge. The crib will have no bottom in it and all water that gets on the inside of this crib will be filtered through about four feet of earth. The crib will then be connected with the well at the water works by a thirty inch iron pipe which will completely shut out the water from Mooney's tannery and other factories and also surface drainage. This work will cost the city about $4,500, at least this is the estimate placed on the cost of this work by Mr. Hege.

Against the completion of this work the votes of McCullough, Rost and Parker were recorded. The council, as it was informed by City Attorney Donaker, had no power to compel the water works trustees to a this work, but it is thought that they will proceed with it.

Taylorsville
The Republic. September 11, 1894 p. 4
Bluford Puris has moved to Columbus from whence he came about a year ago. He has been worthy employee of the Mooney Tannery for many years and removed to Columbus for convenience.

Off Their Trucks
The Republic. November 28, 1894 p. 4
All quiet at Mooney's tannery to-day.

Personal and Society
The Republic. November 29, 1894 p. 4
Charlie Jonee, an employee at Mooney's tannery, had his hand caught in one of the heavy doors of the building yesterday, inflicting a painful wound.

Personal and Society
The Republic. December 7, 1894 p. 4
The little strike at Mooney's tannery, infant as it was, cost the city in the way of extra police service $31. Strikes come high no matter how small they are.

[untitled]
The Republic. January 15, 1895 p. 4
Yesterday morning after Mr. Frank Beatty's little son had brought him into work at the Mooney tannery and returning home, the horse, which attached to a bob-sled, frightened at something, running away, over-turning the sled, throwing the boy off, hurting his back considerably.

Commercial Club
The Republic. March 9, 1895 p. 8
President Kollmeyer called the club to order a o'clock last evening. Roll call showed the following members present: C. J. Kollmeger, P. H. McCormack, Frank Coats, Dr. Heckard, G. W. Caldwell, Frank McNeal, W. H. Dowell, A. Strauss, Edward Mooney,

Dan Crow, Dr. Lopp, H. Tompkins, J. N. Marsh, B. B. Jones, V. L. Grier, Lester Drake, Prof. Harper, C. F. Sparrell, O. M, McCracken, S. E. Haigh. [...]

Presided Kollmeyer said he trusted, all members would refrain from personal abuse and be courteous to one another. [...]

Mr. McCormack said he wanted the water works question taken up. He was in favor of good water, and favored any way to get good water that was deemed by the council best. President Kollmeyer said that he had drawn up several petitions to have a sewer put in; that no one knew better than he did what the citizens of Columbus had to suffer by bad water. The stench from the refuse from the Mooney tannery and starch factory was fearful. He did not blame the Mooneys for it; they operated large plants; contributed largely to the prosperity of the city; but he thought the city should take up the matter of sewerage and do it at their own expense. He had no doubt that this foul sewerage had been the cause of the death of hundreds of citizens of Columbus from typhoid fever contracted from drinking this foul water. He was in hopes that the state board of health would take it up.

A motion of Mr. Coats was made that the club respectfully ask the council to proceed at once to take action to purify the water in the best manner possible. Mr. Mooney did not know whether this would be the proper thing to do or not. Mr. McCormack thought the club ought to suggest not dictate. That the two bodies should cooperate with each other for their best; interests. Mr. McNeal said we have a committee on municipal affairs.

Mr. Caldwell said the council had no power unless they received it under the new law. Mr. Caldwell said if the water-works was moved there would be no use to sewer.

Mr. McCormack thought sewer should be built it it cost $4,000 or $8,000, although he did not think it would cost so much. Mr. Coats said the sewer ought to be put in whether the water-works was moved or not. While he was in the council they put in a sewer but it was not long enough and should be made longer. Upon motion the matter of water-works and sewerage was left to the municipal committee.

Personal and Society
The Republic. July 2, 1895 p. 2
Mr. George Henke, bookkeeper at Mooney's tannery, will leave next month for his old home in Germany.

Personal and Society
The Republic. July 2, 1895 p. 4
J. Worsdall returned home this morning from a business trip for the Mooney tannery.

Many Editors
The Republic. March 27, 1896 p. 6
When the editors assembled for the afternoon session President Packard appointed the following committee on legislation: S. B. Boyd, of the *Washington*

Democrat, S. E. Haigh, of the *Columbus Republican*, and W. W. Aikens, of the Franklin newspaper. [...]

At the Reeves & Co. agricultural implement factory Marshall T. Reeves conducted the party through the works. The Mooney tannery was the next place visited. Mr. Will Mooney showed the party through the largest harness leather tannery in the world, and presented each with a piece of leather made in the factory.

Personal and Society
The Republic. April 8, 1897 p. 4
C. A. Gordon, of Cincinnati, is in the city on business connected with the Mooney tannery.

Asked to Remain Away
The Republic. July 17, 1897 p. 1
Asked to Remain Away. Striking Men at Mooney's Tannery Given Notice to Workmen Claim a Forty per cent Redaction In Wages As the Cause of the Strike — Workingmen Requested to Stay Away Until the Matter is Settled — Done by Order of the Committee.

The workingmen who were formerly in the employ of W. W. Mooney & Sons, tanners, have posted notices requesting all laborers in the country to remain away from the tannery.

The poster reads: Notice is hereby given, that the workmen at Mooney's Tannery, July 12, 1897, did then and there refuse to work and took their tools and walked quietly away from said shop, on account of a forty per cent reduction in wages. Therefore, we, the workmen who walked out of said shop on July 12, 1897, because of said forty per cent reduction of wages do hereby earnestly request all workingmen in the country to not take our places, but to stay until the matter is settled. By order of

COMMITTEE.

This, the 16th day of July, 1897, Columbus. Ind.

This is the first official communication coming from the strikers. The significance of this notice can only be a matter of conjecture. The workmen this afternoon claim that it is only a matter of protection.

Two Workmen Assaulted

The Republic. July 24, 1897 p. 1

Two Workmen Assaulted. John Gilday and W. E. Turner Badly Beaten Last Evening. Trial at the Court House This Afternoon. Done in the Face of an Injunction Issued By Judge Hord — Other Men Are at Work at the Tannery — Change of Public Sentiment.

Samuel Lawless and Walter Kinsel, two of the strikers at Mooney's tannery, were fined for assault and battery on John Gilday and W. E. Turner last evening. John Lawhead was found not guilty. Lawless was fined $5 and costs and Kinsel was fined $1 and costs.

Fighting strikers caused scenes of wild confusion in Columbus last evening. Workingmen who had taken back places in the Mooney tannery were assaulted and beaten. The streets were filled with excited people who talked of the affair until late.

The trouble occurred just after the shops shut down for the day. All day the strikers were conspicuous by their absence from the streets, but about the time for the factory to close small crowds of men gathered in various places.

The workingmen were not assaulted until they had separated and were several blocks from the factory. John Gilday was waylaid near Herman Carr's residence. He had almost reached his home when two strikers, S. Lawless and J. Lawhead, jumped from a buggy, in which two others were sitting, and proceeded to severely beat him. His head was badly cut and his face was almost raw from the pounding he received. He was placed in a carriage and taken to his home. His assailants got back into their buggy and were driven rapidly away.

W E. Turner was also badly injured. He was near the railroad station when the strikers caught him and beat him over the head and face.

Interview With Mr. Gilday.

Mr. Gilday, in regard to the affair, said:

"I expected no trouble whatever even when I saw the men approaching me. I was struck several times with a pair of knucks, knocked down and then kicked. I was not able to work to day, being quite nervous and sore. I want it understood that I did not strike and do not belong to the strikers organization. They have no claim on me whatever. I worked two half days last week and was paid twenty five cents per hour. I took no one's job, but simply kept my own. I refused to take any other man's place. I suppose they thought I was in sympathy with or was encouraging the new workmen which did not do."

Shall Columbus Be the Loser?
The Republic. July 30, 1897 p. 4
Shall Columbus Be the Loser?

Columbus is threatened with the loss of another factory. Are the men who have the welfare of the city at heart to sit idly by and watch the stroke fall without doing so much as to try to avert it? The Mooney Tannery Company has received a number of propositions from other cities and from other States asking this company to come to them. These other cities are offering free land, free gas, free buildings. The gas belt has a number of cities who will do this if this factory will accept their propositions. Newark, N. J., Decatur, Alabama, and many other cities are bidding for this plant.

On the other hand what is Columbus doing to hold the factory here? For what reason should this factory consider itself bound to Columbus? Columbus is supporting free silver papers that are using this difficulty for political purposes. If they told the truth they would say, "Keep up this strike until the tenth of August and then you can do as you please." There are men in this city who are talking against the methods of this company. Talking of this business as one that should not be controlled by the company but by the employees. There are men in this city who would be glad to see that this factory was to leave, as in its leaving their selfish aims and selfish purposes would be subserved. Are they to be allowed to continue?

What is this factory worth to the city of Columbus? Fifty thousand dollars a year is paid in wages. More than $165 a day. What do the business men of Columbus care for this amount? Is it nothing? Is there anything in this city that is of as much value to Columbus as this factory? There is not. And the people know it and the business men know it. And the papers that are using the unadjusted relationship of the employer and the employee to serve the purpose of their party know it. Will they dare say that the factory should go? And yet they are doing all in their power to drive it from us. Will the business men, irrespective of party, affiliations, allow this talk to go farther, or just so sure as this continues the city is to loose. And this will be the result of men who would serve themselves rather than the city.

W. W. Mooney and Sons last fall supported the Republican ticket. This year they are the victims of a political persecution because they did so. And it is malicious, malevolent persecution. Let the men of Columbus look squarely at this situation. Consider what this blow would mean. For it would be a blow that would tell and that deeply. And then if they are to let this set of men, not the employees, but a set of small politicians, who would ruin this city for their own gain, proceed with their work, the blame will be on themselves. It is in their hands to stop this work and at once.

Personal
The Republic. August 12, 1897 p. 8
Frank Huffman, one of the striking workmen at Mooney's Tannery, has gone to St. Louis to accept a position.

[untitled]
The Republic. August 12, 1897 p. 4
Fred Rethwisch, one of the striking workmen of Mooney's Tannery, left yesterday for Indianapolis and Chicago in search of a position.

Wind Rain and Fire
The Republic. January 24, 1898 p. 1
Wind, Rain and Fire Combined to Make Saturday Night One of Terror. Mooney's Tannery and the Big Four Beer House Burned — Much Damage to Property — Electric Wires Down.

Wind, rain and fire combined to make Saturday night one of terror to the people of Columbus. Falling showers of burning embers made the people believe that all property lying within a radius of a mile of the Mooney tannery, where the hair house was burning, would certainly be destroyed. The wheat elevator, leased by H. Griffith, was in danger, and it was thought that if the elevator was fired the results would be disastrous to the business portion of the city.

Following the rain of Saturday, which raised all the streams and creeks and rivers, shortly after darkness came a wind arose. This continued to increase in velocity until by 10 o'clock a gale was blowing.

Signs and awnings fell. Storm doors, chimneys, roofs and fences lay scattered about the city as if a cyclone was passing. Those whose duties kept them out of doors hurried through their work and hastened to their homes. Those at home waited for the belated ones and even after they came remained up waiting for the end. The end did not come until the morning's light came to show the wreckage that the wind had piled up.

The climax of the terror came when at 1:30 o'clock in the morning the fire alarm was sounded. The central station of the telephone companies reported Mooney's tannery was on fire and the horror was increased.

The first alarm was soon followed by the call for all firemen. Then the sky grew bright. The fire department drove down Fifth street at a swift speed to Jackson, where it was saved much trouble and probably a wreck by Policeman Ferguson who gave the warning in time to save the drivers from dashing into a pile of poles and wires which the storm had piled up at Fifth and Jackson streets.

At the tannery the hair house was burned. This caught probably from the steam pipes. The loss is about $600, fully insured. The sparks, still burning, blew all over the city. Only the drenched roofs saved a general conflagration. The burnt building was seperate from the main factory. It was about thirty feet square.

One peculiar feature showed the velocity of the wind, was the fact that citizens in the northern and eastern portion of the city, smelt the burning hair before the alarm was turned in. In many houses so strong was the odor that people got up and made an investigation, thinking that something was burning upon their premises. This was noticed at the home of Mr. Samuel Beam, who resides east of the city, and nearly four miles from the scene of the fire.

Before the people were asleep again another alarm was sounded. This time the beer house, owned by Henry Palmer, was burning, caught from the Mooney fire. The loss here was about $7 with no insurance.

Telegraph companies suffered more than the telephone companies. For a time there was no communication with Louisville or Madison. One hundred and fifty-seven poles were blown down between Jonesville and Louisville and 126 between Columbus and Madison. Fencing all over the county suffered.

The river rose steadily all day yesterday but today it is falling and the worst is past.

Large Well Being Dug
The Republic. June 2, 1898 p. 4
What will be when completed the largest well in this county and surrounding country is now being dug at Mooney's tannery. The well is fourteen feet in diameter and will be fifty-five feet deep when completed. Its capacity will be 200,000 gallons per hour.

A Desperate Encounter

The Republic. June 15, 1898 p. 4

A Desperate Encounter. Leoti Gable Shot, Badly Hurt, While Resisting Arrest. Wholesale Place of Thievery Brought to Light — Large Amount of Stolen Goods Found.

[...] Gable admits to the thieving he is charged with. He has stolen large amounts of goods from Lehman & Co. and Campbell, Boyd & Co.'s store. The affair took place between 4 o'clock and 5 o'clock this morning.

About 4 o'clock John Haislup, who had gone to Mooney's Tannery to get his working clothes, as he was to do some other work to-day, saw Gable in Campbell, Boyd & Co.'s wholesale grocery store. He reported the fact to the police and he started at once on Gable's trail. He had a wagon near the store and, in the meantime had gotten to it and was driving toward the eastern part of the city, when the police were notified.

Wounded at Santiago

The Republic. July 5, 1898 p. 2

Walter Kinson was wounded in the left ankle during the engagement before Santiago recently. Kinson formerly lived in this city and was employed at Mooney's tannery. His brother, Gus, resides on Brown street.

Walter Kinsel at Santiago

The Republic. July 6, 1898 p. 4

Walter Kinsel, formerly of this city, was wounded in the recent battle at Santiago. Kinsel worked at Mooney's tannery while in this city but left here after the strike at that place last summer to join a regiment of the regular army then stationed in North Dakota. The Associated Press dispatches yesterday gave his name as Walter Kinson, Company G. Sixteenth U. S. Infantry, but there can be no doubt but that Walter Kinsel is meant since he belonged to the above company and regiment.

Ed Lawhead Missing

The Republic. July 14, 1898 p. 4

Ed Lawhead Missing. An Employee of W. W. Mooney & Son's Tannery Does Not Show Up.

Ed Lawhead, formerly an employed at the Mooney Tannery and recently employed at their works at Louisville is missing.

Mr. Lawhead worked at Mooney's for many years and was one of the leaders of the strike there last July. When the strike was declared off he went back to work but was, sent to the tannery at Louisville and since that time, until about a week ago, he has been a worker there.

His wife and children have lived here all this time. About a week ago he told them, by mail, that he had been offered a better position at Scottsburg and that he had quit at Louisville. The household goods were to be packed and sent to Scottsburg on his arrival here. He did not arrive Monday and on Tuesday his wife shipped the goods, expecting to hear from him any hour.

She and the children are still here staying with friends but up to date not word has been received concerning Lawhead. His wife entertains grave doubts as to his whereabouts, but an old friend of his in this city thinks that he has joined the army.

Walter Kinsel at Ft. Thomas
The Republic. July 19, 1898 p. 4
Walter Kinsel at Ft. Thomas. One of the Soldiers Injured in the Battle Before Santiago.

Walter Kinsel, of Company G. 16th Regiment Infantry of U. S. regulars, who was wounded at Santiago, is now at Ft. Thomas, KY. Kinsel was in the thickest of the fight, his company being stationed nearest Teddy Roosevelt's rough riders. Kinsel suffered a wound in the ankle and had three fingers on the right hand shot off. An Associated Press dispatch says that his wounds are in no manner dangerous and he is recovering rapidly. His brother, Augustus, residing in this city, has telegraphed the authorities at Ft. Thomas, asking that Walter Kinsel be brought here. He had received no answer at two o'clock this afternoon.

Walter Kinsel is well known here. He was one of the strikers at Mooney's Tannery last summer, and refusing to go to work, went west and enlisted in the regular army.

Position at Tannery
The Republic. July 25, 1898 p. 2
John Scott, Jr. has been made assistant chemist at the Mooney Tannery. This place was made vacant by Edwin Cobb joining the Columbus Company.

Police Court News
The Republic. September 15, 1898 p. 3
[...] John Davis, who works at Mooney's tannery and was charged as an accomplice in stealing a horse from Jake Hughes, August 6, was brought before Squire Stader this afternoon for trial. On account of an absent witness the case was continued until Sept. 29, at 2 o'clock.

Business Paragraphs
The Republic. November 12, 1898 p. 4
Samuel Wright, formerly a worker in the Mooney tannery, who has been in Massillon, Ohio, for almost a year, has returned to this city and is again engaged at Mooney's.

Personal Paragraphs
The Republic. January 13, 1899 p. 4
Will Keyes arrived last evening from Winchester, Ky., to make Columbus his future residence. Mr. Keyes will be engaged at the Mooney tannery.

Society Events
The Republic. January 21, 1899 p. 2
Rumor has it that a quiet little wedding will occur to-morrow, the participants being a young man from

Ohio employed at Mooney's tannery and a prominent young society lady of this city.

[untitled]
The Republic. May 30, 1899 p. 4
The storm of yesterday evening did no especial damage in the city so far as reported. At Mooney's tannery the top of one of the tall smoke stacks was blown off.

[untitled]
The Republic. June 6, 1899 p. 4
Wesley Rudolph, Garden City, was the guest of his father, Jeremiah Rudolph, of Beck, part of last week. Wesley is an employee at Mooney's tannery.

[untitled]
The Republic. June 28, 1899 p. 4
Elmer Moore will lose a finger nail the result of getting a sliver under it at Mooney's tannery this morning.

Is Not Sustained
The Republic. July 7, 1899 p. 4
Railroad Ordinance Passed Over; the Mayor's Veto to Advertise for Bids. The Mill Race and California and Seventh Street Sewers to be Built — A Long, and Tedious Session of the City Council Last Night — The Claims.

[...] On motion of Reeves, the clerk was instructed to advertise for bids for construction of the mill race sewer and the California and Seventh streets sewer.

McCormack objected to the mill race sewer being extended beyond the Mooney tannery upon the ground that its extension beyond that point is unnecessary unless the proposed Eighth street sewer is built. Dryden thought different and said it would be but a short time until that sewer would be built; that most of the property owners would demand it. McCormack's objection went for naught, and bids will be advertised for the construction of the sewer as first contemplated, from the water works to a point on Washington street where the Glanton ditch crosses. Upon the roll call all the councilmen but McCormack voted aye on the motion of Reeves as above. In connection with the sewer matter it was reported that the Big Four railway company grants permission to put sewer under railroad tracks where necessary. [...]

Arm Dislocated

The Republic. July 22, 1899 p. 4

Will Carry, employed at Mooney's tannery, fell from a bark-pile yesterday evening and dislocated bis arm. Dr. MacCoy attended the injury.

Wright Prather

The Republic. September 12, 1899 p. 4

The marriage of Miss Littie Prather to Mr. Samuel Wright took place at their home near the Methodist church Sunday morning at 8 o'clock, the Rev. E. B. Widger performing the ceremony. The bride is the third daughter of Mr. and Mrs. T. B. Prather. The groom is an employee at Mooney's tannery.

Personal Points
The Republic. September 19, 1899 p. 2
Joseph H. Griffis, who was formerly at Mooney's tannery, but who now is a resident of Cambridge City, is in the city to-day transacting business.

[untitled]
The Republic. September 25, 1899 p. 4
George Brockman assumes the duties of mailing clerk at Mooney's tannery to-day.

A Heel Factory
The Republic. February 20, 1900 p. 4
T. F. Robinson, of New York, has opened a small factory at the end of Fourth street where he will manufacture shoe heels from the offal leather of Mooney's tannery. His enterprise is backed by several Columbus business men.

A Gang of School Boys
The Republic. February 21, 1900 p. 4
Have a Den In Cramp's Brick Yard Near The River, Where They Smoke, Swear, and Play Cards.

   A gang of about one dozen boys have erected a brick house at Crump's old brickyard, west of the Mooney tannery and they "play hookey" from school occasionally, and congregate at their improvised home. A man investigated their premises the other day and found about eight boys present, all smoking, swearing, and playing cards, a big roaring fire burning in one corner of their house. They are reported to steal food, etc., away from home and take it to this place and cook it. The boys are the sons of respectable parents, and it is believed that the visit of the truant officer to their den would break up this social enterprise of theirs.

Notice
The Republic. March 8, 1900 p. 4
Employees of Money's Tannery will please meet at nine o'clock to-morrow morning at the tannery for the purpose of arranging to attend the funeral W. Mooney.

With the Sick
The Republic. April 30, 1900 p. 2
G. L. Reeves and little son, Robert, are on the sick list.

Frank Mosbaugh, chemist at Mooney's tannery, who has been quite sick, is convalescent.

Personal Points
The Republic. June 8, 1900 p. 4
J. MacKain left this morning for Pennsylvania, in interest of Mooney's Tannery.

Personal Points
The Republic. September 3, 1900 p. 4
Clarence Grove left Saturday evening for New York in the interest of Mooney's tannery.

Through the South
The Republic. October 8, 1900 p. 2
Will Curry, travelling salesman for W. W. Mooney & Sons tannery, left last evening for the south in the interests of the Mooney tannery.

A New Tanning Firm
The Republic. October 24, 1900 p. 4
John Thompson and Dan Greenfield, Jr., have organized a fur dressing and tanning company, with their shops in East Columbus. They are prepared to do fancy tanning. Both are experienced workmen having been in the employ of the Mooney tannery for many years.

An Extended Trip
The Republic. October 30, 1900 p. 4
Miss Loa Gray, stenographer at the Mooney Tannery office, will leave to-morrow for an extended trip through northern Indiana and the east.

A Beautiful Piece of Work
The Republic. December 3, 1900 p. 4
One of the most beautiful pieces of workmanship in the tanning art can be seen in the shop of W. F. Miller, the harness man at 221 South Washington street. John A. Hack, a farmer, who lives 41 miles southwest of town has two cow hides tanned, one a Holstein the other a brindle Jersey, on exhibition, the Holstein being a beautiful piece of work. Mr. Hack at one time worked at the Mooney Tannery in

this city. The Holstein hide is valued at $25, and is combination of black and dark cream.

Child Burned to Death
The Republic. December 17, 1900 p. 4
In East Columbus by Her Clothing Catching Fire. Mother Left Three-Year-Old Girl Alone For a Few Minutes and When She Returned the Child Was Horribly Burned.

Ruth Wilson, the little three and one-half year old daughter of Mr. and Mrs. Samuel Wilson, of East Columbus, died at 5 o'clock Sunday morning from the result of burns received Saturday night. Mrs. Wilson was baking some bread in a neighbor's stove Saturday night and about 9 o'clock had left her own home to go and see about the bread. She left her child alone in the house. When she returned she found her child's clothing enveloped in flames and the little one crying piteously. The child was horribly burned and medical attention could do little towards alleviating the extreme pain. She died about eight hours later.

The manner in which the child's clothing caught fire is not exactly known but it is supposed that she was playing with paper near the fire. The mother had not been gone over a few minutes when the child's clothing was in flames. The father of the little girl is employed at Mooney's tannery.

The funeral will take place from the family home in East Columbus at 1 o'clock Tuesday afternoon, at 2 o'clock from the Clifty German Lutheran church,

Rev. George Fisher officiating. Interment at Clifty cemetery.

Short Session of Council

The Republic. December 21, 1900 p. 4

Mooney & Sons' Tannery Given a Two-cent Rate for Water. Mooney Ask to Be Treated Like Other Manufactures in Regard to Exemption From Taxes.

The City Council met in regular session last night. Mayor Caldwell and Councilman Williams were absent. P. H. McCormack was called to preside, upon the motion of Reeves.

[...] Kelble, of the water works committee, reported that a rate of 2 cents per 1,000 gallons had been recommended for Mooney's tannery for a period of ten years.

William A. Mooney, secretary and treasurer of the Mooney plant, was present and spoke to the council. He thanked them for the rate made for water and said that the same was thankfully received. Mr. Mooney stated that there was one manufactory here that had been exempted from taxation and had been given free water for ten years and that another manufactory had been exempted from one half of the taxation and also free water. He said that all they asked was to be treated like other manufacturers. "We have made considerable improvements at our plant in recent years," said Mr. Mooney, "and have employed more men. We expect to make more improvements and to employ still more men, but this depends altogether on what this council does. If discrimination is to be made we do not propose to further push our energies toward building up this city. We expect to enlarge either here or elsewhere."

Kelble's motion for a 2 cent rate for Mooney's (one-half of the present rate) was adopted all voting aye except Dryden, who voted no because the motion did not include all manufactures in the city.

Emmons thought that if other manufactures were exempted from taxation that Mooney should be also. Thomas Mooney, the senior member of the Mooney tannery firm, was also present and made a few pointed remarks. He said that no discrimination should be made. All manufactures should be treated alike. He said that his firm wanted the same exemption as others had received or they did not propose to stay here.

Emmons moved, supported by Carr, that Mooney's be exempted of one-half of their taxes for a period of 10 years. Tormehlen thought that time should be taken to consider the question. Reeves moved to refer the matter to the finance committee and the motion carried.

City Council's Brisk Session
The Republic. January 18, 1901 p. 4
Mooney and Schinnerer Will Be Furnished With Free Water. The Question of Buying Hose for the Fire Department Was Settled this Morning — Other Business Transactions.

Although the business session of the city council was short last night, some important matters were disposed of. Among the most important things up before this honorable body for consideration were the Mooney Tannery tax reduction and the placing of an order for about 1,000 feet of fire hose.

[...] Councilmen Carr, Emmons and McBride with whom was left the matter of furnishing free water to Mooney & Sons, reported in favor, of that proposition in order to equalize that firm with the Reeves Pulley Co. and Reeves & Co., but recommended that the firm pay their own taxes. In a motion to adopt, Reeves was supported by Carr, Dryden and Williams voted nay but the motion carried just the same.

Personal Points
The Republic. February 27, 1901 p. 4
John Worsdall, of Georgia, was in the city yesterday on business. Mr. Worsdall was a former employee of The Mooney Tannery.

The Entire City at a Standstill
The Republic. March 5, 1901 p. 4
Fire Started in Wine Room of Henry and Smith's Saloon. High Pressure Of Water Burst The Main Near The Water Works And Inconvenienced Factories, Hotels, And Private Families.

At 1:30 o'clock this morning an alarm from box 14 brought the fire department to the rear of the buildings occupied by Henry & Smiths as a saloon and Ernst Stahlhuth as a drug store. Fire was seen issuing from the structure and before the blaze could be extinguished about $1,000 damage was done.

Henry & Smith are the heaviest losers, the drug store being only slightly damaged.

[...] The rupture in the water main has caused more loss and inconvenience to Columbus than the fire did. With the exception of a very few, all factories were forced to close down, because of not having water with which to make steam, throwing almost two thousand mechanics and laborers out of work temporarily. Those not effected are the Columbus Handle and Tool Company and the Mooney tannery, which institutions use water from wells. In an interview with one of the officials of the Mooney Co., it was learned that there were some doubts as to whether their supply of water would hold out.

The Hopper
The Republic. May 6, 1901 p. 2
Ellis Hunter and wife will soon move to New York to reside in the future. Mr. Hunter goes east to take charge of the eastern branch of the Mooney tannery.

Municipalies Meet Jointly
The Republic. May 8, 1901 p. 2
Eighth Session of the Municipal League at City Hall. The Attendance is All That Was Expected and the Visitors are Being Treated Royally — The Ladies' Session.

[...] At 1:30 o'clock this afternoon the Municipal League was called to order in the City Hall by Hon Z. T. Dungan, mayor of Huntington, Ind. He made a few brief complimentary remarks after which invocation was offered by Rev. A. J. Frank, pastor of the Tabernacle. The address of welcome was then delivered by Hon. George W. Caldwell, mayor of Columbus. His welcome was a hearty one and is as follows:

[...] Allow me to remind you that our city is located on the beautiful White River Valley and at the beginning of the celebrated Hawpatch of Indiana. This county was named for General Bartholomew, and this city was laid out by General Tipton, Both are personages well known as having taken a great part in making the early history of Indiana. The first railroad west of the Alleghany mountains was built from Madison, Ind., to this city, and is the third oldest railroad in the United States. The old J. M. & I, its first engines were built in England, shipped to Baltimore, and carried in pieces by pack mules over the Alleghany mountains to Pittsburgh, and from there were floated down the Ohio river to Madison, Ind. We have many manufactories, some of which are worthy of especial mention, such as Mooney's tannery, the largest harness leather tannery in the United States: the Orinoco tannery, Reeves & Co, one of the largest threshing machine manufacturers in the state: the Reeves Pulley Co, the home of the speed varying mechanism; the Orinoco and Glanton furniture factories which are noted for their superior furniture products, and other industries too numerous to mention. You are especially invited to visit these places while with us. In conclusion permit me to call your attention to the public utilities owned and operated by our city. Columbus owns her own water works system, electric light system, Gamewell fire alarm system, paid fire department, and her own city hall. Again extending you the courtesies of our city, I remain yours to command.

The Lightning Does a Few Turns
The Republic. June 21, 1901 p. 4
Took a Smash at Mooney's Tannery Thursday Evening. Home of Herman Carr on Sycamore Street was Stricken and Considerable Damage was Perpetrated as a Result.

Shortly after 11 o'clock Thursday night the fire department was called to the home of Hermann Carr, between Seventh and Eighth street, where fire had originated. The origin of the fire is supposed to be in the lightning which prevailed a greater part of last night and to-day. The fire started in the smoke house and by the time the fire department arrived the flames were making much headway. The alarm was turned in by Anderson Shultz. It was not long after the arrival of the apparatus that the flames were under control and in an hour the fire was out. The total loss to the house will reach $500, fully insured.

Another prank played by the lightning was the destruction of the smoke stack at the Mooney tannery. At this place the roof of the building was also damaged and the total amount of destruction will probably reach $500, fully covered by insurance. The roof, where the lightning struck, looks as though it had been hit with a shot gun loaded with slags. The stack was totally destroyed.

Considerable damage was perpetrated by the storm through the county but nothing of a serious nature was experienced outside of the two misfortunes stated above. All last night and part of to-day heavy rains have been falling and according to the predictions more rains and thunder storms will prevail to-night. Saturday will be clear.

Reports from the surrounding towns are to the effect that pyrotechnics played all over the country. At the telephone exchanges at some points the board had to be abandoned but no damage was done.

The Hopper
The Republic. June 26, 1901 p. 4
Elmer Moore left this morning for Lima, Oh., where he has accepted a good position in the tannery there. For some time Mr. Moore has been employed at the Mooney tannery as a buffer. His many friends in Columbus wish him all possible success.

Personal Points
The Republic. July 26, 1901 p. 2
Clarence Grove, of the New York branch establishment of the Mooney Tannery, is here on a short vacation.

The Hopper
The Republic. August 10, 1901 p. 4
At noon while Frank Smith, bookkeeper at Mooney's tannery, was going home to dinner he stumbled and fell on some boards near Dr. Rice's residence. His shins were skinned, an ankle was sprained and he was otherwise jolted and bruised.

The Hopper
The Republic. October 14, 1901 p. 4
Charles Leper, fireman at Mooney's tannery, fell against the brick wall supporting the boilers at that place Sunday and sustained a gash on the right side of his head. He was rendered unconscious for a time. Dr. Arnold was called and gave the injured man the necessary attention.

Meeting Will Be Brilliant
The Republic. November 25, 1901 p. 4
Everything in Readiness to Receive the Press Association. Banquet Program is Made. The Editors Will Be Escorted About the City and Will be Shown all the Points of Interest — Prizes Offered.

[...] Carriages to start from the city hall, going north on Franklin street to Twelfth, east on Twelfth to Sycamore, north on Sycamore to Sixteenth, thence by shortest route through Northside and Orinoco to the Orinoco tannery, where the party will inspect the tannery. From there back to the Orinoco furniture factory, thence to Glanton's furniture factory, thence to the Columbus Handle & Tool Company, thence to

Reeves Pulley factory, then to Reeves & Co.'s factory on Fifth street. From there west on Fifth to Pearl, north on Pearl to Twelfth, west on Twelfth to Washington and the Sanitarium, south on Washington to Fifth, west on Fifth to Mooney's tannery. After inspecting the Mooney tannery the company will drive south on Brown to the new power house. Thence to the National Machine Works, east on Second to Washington, and thence to the city hall.

Press Members Tour the City
The Republic. November 26, 1901 p. 4
Fall Meeting of Southern Indiana Press Association. A Big Banquet Planned. A Slight Change Made in The Time of Giving the Programs — A Number of Indiana Writers to Arrive Tonight.

[...] This afternoon at 1 o'clock the visitors and quite & number of prominent citizens, members of the Columbus Commercial Club, gathered at the city hall, in front of which pretty building were drawn up about 8 dozen carriages, including a buck-board. The citizens and visitors stepped into the vehicles and were taken on a tour, the points of interest being the many substantial institutions in all quarters of the city. The route taken by the procession was as follows: From the city hall, north on Franklin street to Twelfth, west on Twelfth to Sycamore, north on Sycamore to Sixteenth, thence by shortest route through Northside and Orinoco to the Orinoco tannery, where the party will inspect the tannery. From there back to the Orinoco furniture factory, thence to

Glanton's furniture factory, thence to the Columbus Handle & Tool Company, thence to Reeves Pulley factory, then to Reeves & Co.'s' factory on Fifth street. From there west on Fifth to Pearl, north on Pearl to Twelfth, west on Twelfth to Washington and the Sanitarium, south on Washington to Fifth, west on Fifth to Mooney's tannery. After inspecting the Mooney tannery the company will drive south on Brown to the new power house. Thence to the National Machine Works, east on Second to Washington, and thence to the city hall.

The City's Growth
The Republic. November 27, 1901 p. 3
Speech Delivered by G. L. Reeves at the Editors Banquet.

The following interesting speech was made by Gurney L. Reeves, at the banquet given Tuesday evening to the Southern Indiana Press Association given by the Commercial club of Columbus:

Mr. Toastmaster, Ladies and Gentlemen of the Southern Indiana Editorial Association:

It was my special request that I be permitted to speak after the distinguished gentleman to whom you have just listened. The very nature of my subject and my own capabilities preclude absolutely the faintest suggestion of oratory, and I well knew that when our silver tongued attorneys and the illustrious out-of-town orators had concluded their perorations, their would be no magnolia blooms to gather, as murmuring brooklets to murmur; there would be no sun-kissed peaks to peek, and nary a star left unpawed: and that with all these trivialities out of the way and disposed of, I could proceed directly to my subject. I never attend a function of this kind and contemplate an uneven hitch-up of windy lawyers, good speakers and "beefy rubes" from the lowly walks of life, that I do not think of the conscientious and somewhat resourceful deacon, who was the owner of a quite muscular although perniciously stubborn bell-calf. The calf refused to work, and the deacon, thinking to teach him an impressive lesson in humility and straightforwardness of conduct, yoked himself up with the calf. It is needless to say something happened, and as the deacon and the calf went flying down the dirt road toward the little village at Lake Shore Limited speed, both together touching only the high places, the deacon managed to yell out — "Fools of perdition, stop us!" The villagers soon formed a bank of humanity and brought the couple to a standstill and proceeded to disengage and disentangle. Between gravel and sand expectorations, puffs and perhaps something worse, the deacon gasped — "Never mind me, unyoke the calf. I'll stand."

And so I feel to-night. You have been hitched to such a flight of oratory that you will be glad to sit still while I just talk a little. Columbus has manufacturing industries — this shall be my theme. In the brief time allotted to me this evening, it will be quite impossible to enter any accurate or detailed historical account of any individual manufacturing institution, but rather treat them collectively. The manufacturing interest of Columbus dates from 1853, when Wm. Brinkley built a factory on what is now the corner of Sycamore and Sixth street, for the manufacture of furniture. This factory Mr. Brinkley operated uninterruptedly until his death, in 1897. About ten years later, the Mooney tannery was moved to this city, and almost contemporaneous with it came the woolen mill; then the wheel company; and, in 1876, Reeves & Company; a year or two later, the Cerealine Manufacturing Company, and almost at the same time, the Starch Works: then Mr. Jas. A. Glanton began the manufacture of furniture; later came the Orinoco Furniture Co., Columbus Handle & Tool Co., Reeves Pulley Co., Orinoco tanning Co., the Canning factory, the Saddlery Co., and other institutions. I do not know that I have these all in their regular order, or that the dates are exactly correct, but think they are practically so.

In the Columbus of to-day we see quite a lively manufacturing center. I was rather pleasantly surprised myself, upon investigation, to find the volume so large. Columbus employs approximately 1,600 men, to whom she pays annually $650,000, and the product of whose handiwork represents the enormous sum total of at least $4,000,000. Its products include furniture, leather, canned goods, threshing machinery, power transmission machinery, handles, harness, oils, flour, brick, and are marketed not only in the United States, Canada and Mexico, but Europe, South America and far away Australia. South Africa, China, Japan and New Zealand know and appreciate and buy goods manufactured in the bustling little city whose guests you are this evening. At the heads of its different industries (with but a few notable exceptions) are men aggressive, alert, with an ambition for a broader attainment in their respective lines.

In the investigations of our manufacturing interests of Columbus, one of the notable and, in my opinion, most commendable impressions is the uniformly high grade of the goods produced. We have not, within our borders, a single institution, in so far as I know, marketing what is known as "cheap" goods. The furniture built in this city is seen in the windows of the fashionable Fifth Avenue dealer of New York, who caters to the "exclusive set." The famous "Mooney Pure Oak-tanned Hand-Stuffed Leather" is the stock to which the dealer refers when he says he has "something just as good." It represents the highest attainment of the tanner's art; it is the high water mark by which other leathers are gauged. Columbus handles are known to both American and European markets for the uniform excellency of the grade. The highest priced threshing machinery in the United States is made in Columbus. This significant fact is certainly true of wood-split pulleys and power transmission machinery and appliances, and the other lines of manufacture of the city. It means that, not content with making something just as good, our efforts are to produce absolutely the best: it means the best class of mechanics in their respective lines, and, consequently, the highest market price for labor. Another fact not to be overlooked is, that the commercial industries of Columbus are on a sound financial basis; inflated stocks and exaggerated statements play no part in their conduct. All the lines manufactured are standard staple articles of commodity.

We have no airship plants, and but few perpetual motion cranks. Columbus has never had what might be termed a "boom." It has no natural gas, excepting such as nature has implanted in the tongue-tips of some of its natives. It has not even a copious supply of salt water. It has only recently had a commercial club with any snap or push or promise of longevity. It has, moreover, a multitude of fossilized barnacles, who, most unfortunately for its progress, own quite an amount of its suburban property. And yet, despite all these hinderances, Columbus has had steady growth, and bids fair to amount and survive its every adversary, and to become, within a very few years, a city of at least double its present size, provided, always, that Dave Brunswick lives and a hamstring does not break.

It is not perhaps within the province of my subject that I should refer to any of the external conditions and influences which have gone to make up our past and present as a manufacturing city, and yet I feel you will pardon me if I digress sufficiently to make mention of a man whose life has been so interwoven with our progress and prosperity, that no review, however brief, of our manufacturing, or, indeed, commercial interests, would be complete without his mention. In June, of 1846, a sturdy young man, just arrived at the age of maturity, came trudging into Columbus, having walked down from Edinburg. He could have ridden on the train his mother had given him 30 cents, in the morning, and this was the price of a railroad ticket from Edinburg to Columbus; but upon revolving the matter over in his mind, the young man concluded that perhaps he should want to take advantage of some speculation and would need that 30 cents, and as it happened to be the only 30 cents he had, he would hold onto it and walk. And so, when he bowed his introduction to this then struggling little frontier village, we are talking about, his assets were 30 cents in cash, a little bundle of clothes, a good appetite and a clear conscience. He entered the employ of Snyder & Alden, as a clerk, and out of the meager salary, he saved $150 the first three years — not a large sum, but it would buy three acres of land, and he not only invested the $150, but borrowed enough to bring the amount up to $1,500, and with this he bought a small farm. And then began the task of planting Columbus on his farm.

Very early he learned the lesson that a manufacturing plant is an excellent fertilizer for raising a good healthy town crop on a farm, and he began to encourage them. He sold them sites at most reasonable prices, and on terms they could easily meet if he could not sell them the sites, he gave it to them, and if this was not sufficient he would add thereto a liberal cash bonus; he backed them with his capital; he advised them wisely; and yet, strange and astonishing as it may seem to some of the aforementioned family of "barnacles," who are holding factory sites at $1,000 per acre, and who would pass from one paroxysm to another should a donation be asked, this reckless spendthrift prospered — yes, fourfold and a thousand fold, until to-day his varied and extensive interests touch directly or indirectly, almost every commercial and industrial undertaking in this city and community. And the name of Joseph I. Irwin is a synonym to our people not alone of a Gibraltar rock of financial stability, but as a safe counselor, a generous philanthropist, a citizen to whom we point with pride, and to whom we are much indebted. Other men, not actively interested in manufacturing, but who have contributed much in thought and money to its prosperity, might be mentioned. We have a mayor, a gentleman of whom any city might be proud, a comparatively young man, who has sprung into national prominence in his chosen life work as a contractor and builder; a man who has this city's interest at heart, and who believes in manufactories. The pity of it all is, his immense and varied interests prevent him visiting as as often as we should like. We would fain see more of him.

It would be a rank injustice to pass by the distinguished president our commercial club. His untiring efforts in behalf of the factories is well known and the club under whose auspices this banquet is spread could not have selected a more aggressive and acceptable president than the Hon. P. H. McCormack. Our council chamber is filled at the present time with men who believe in looking into every interest of the manufacturer, and let any factory in Columbus make a reasonable request and it will be granted; and, brothers of the manufacturing fraternity, let us see to it that we make only reasonable requests of them. We have a press who, by constant pounding and rasping and burnishing, are trying to the utmost extent of their ability to clear the ship's sides of the barnacles, so that we may grow and push toward into still greater prominence and usefulness.

A word to our manufacturers: Let as stand shoulder to shoulder for Columbus; let as work in perfect harmony for its interest; and let there be no discord in the family circle. As manufacturers we send this parting message to you, gentlemen: To any substantial manufacturing industry contemplating a change of location, should you choose to cast your lot with us, you will be treated right; you will have unsurpassed shipping facilities; you will have cheap fuel: you will have splendid fire protection; you will have good banking accommodations; you will have as clean and well built and well mannered a little city to live in as you can find in the middle west. If you behave yourself and work hard. you will prosper and be happy, and we stand ready to sound the bugle for your triumphial entry.

Gentlemen, I thank you.

January Wedding
The Republic. November 29, 1901 p. 2

Mr. George Dalgetta-Kerr, of Damascus, Va., and Miss Wall, of Winchester, Va., will be married January second. Miss Wall, who is a young woman of grace and culture, is from one of Virginia's oldest and best families. Mr. Kerr was formerly chemist of the Mooney tannery, and now holds the responsible position of superintendent of one of the largest extract factories of the south.

Our Contemporaries Write About Columbus
The Republic. November 30, 1901 p. 2

C. S. Mercer of Seymour Wants That Prize.

C. S. Mercer, editor of the *Seymour Democrat*, wants the $25 prize offered by the Columbus Commercial Club for the best write up of this city. His impression of our city is as follows:

As we weather the capes of a new century, the query, Did Christopher Columbus discover America? is still an open question. We don't know. We do know that on a recent neighborly visit, with other members of the Southern Indiana Press Association, to Columbus, Ind., we found, hard by the center of population of the United States, a very lively city of living people. A city of five buildings, with convenient appointments, of clean streets, with neat walks on the side, of comfortable homes, of excellent schools, of prosperous churches, of numerous manufactories and of many newspapers — a city of business, with its banner hanging over the outer walls and bearing on its front the legend, "Prosperity," and on the reverse the motto that tells the story of the town, "We Help Ourselves." The metropolis of a broad expanse of the richest and most productive lands in Indiana, it is a city with the unique distinctions of fostering the largest tannery in the world; of having, perhaps, the sole church house in America, or in all the universe for anything we know, with a roof garden annex: of being the only city of comparative size in the state that owns its water works system, self sustaining, with a new power house soon to be completed at a cost of $25,000, its own electric light and power plant and its own city hall, with a well paid, strongly equipped and very effective fire department, including an up-to-date electric alarm system. A city with a magnificent court house, with comparatively the least debt and the lowest tax rate of any corporation of equal and greater population in the state of Indiana, with one single exception a city with an ideal orphans' home, and an independent telephone system, that reaches more people, gives better service and at cheaper rates than any competitor in any Indiana city of equal population; and a plan of sanitation including sewerage, the disposal of all garbage and the supplying of an abundance of pure water that is only equalled in cleverness of planning by the competence of its working; a city proud of being the home of a citizen, the leader in every public enterprise, a promoter of every good cause, a patron of benevolence, and the one man in all the world who individually owns, controls and operates a line of electric street railway that accommodates every portion of the city and reaches to all the boundaries of its suburbs. Withal, a community very strong in commercial interests and manufacturing enterprises, with a population approximating closely the 10,000 mark, with 3,000 people employed in applied mechanics, and a yearly output of manufactured products valued at $4,000,000. A city with two railways — the Pennsylvania and the Big Four — each one of the very best equipped and most accommodating lines in the country, leading to all parts of the Union; and a very near and sure prospect of a connection with the Southern Indiana by a branch line from Azalia. Incidental to the meeting of the Press Association, the members were escorted in carriages by prominent citizens on a general tour of the city and its many and varied industries. The first in order of inspection, the Orinoco tanning Co., in existence only six years, has grown to a plant employing fifty workmen who earn $30,000 annually, and making a leather output valued at $225,000 year. The Orinoco Furniture Co. makes on an exceedingly large scale only furniture of the very highest grade in material, workmanship and finish, which finds an active demand in all the best markets. The unique machinery and finished products of this plant were objects of great interest to the visitors. The factory of the Reeves Pulley Co,. erected in 1890, is operated in the construction of the Reeves Wood Split Pulley, of world-wide fame and worth, and the Reeves Variable Speed Transmission, by which any range of speed can be made, and by which the Franklin Institute gold medal for merit has been awarded. This plant employs 200 men and an annual output has a value of $250,000. Reeves & Co., manufacturers of threshing machines, straw stackers, and saw mills, has a plant covering over five acres, a magnificent equipment, 500 employees, an annual output of $1,125,000 and a business that reaches out to all the boundaries of the commercial world. The Glanton Furniture Co., the Columbus Handle & Tool Co. and the National Machine Works, each having a large plant, fine equipment, a strong force of employees, an extensive and valuable output, and all enjoying a large reputation for the quality and quantity of their products, which find ready sale over a wide field, were visited in turn. The last and greatest establishment visited was the Mooney Tannery, the very largest in the world, making from the raw material every grade of leather known to the trade, in quantity, quality and variety, unapproached by the product of any other industry of its kind, commanding a traffic that extends to every civilized nation and controlling a business world wide in extension.

Within the limits and scope of this article, mention of these industries and other enterprises is, of necessity, more in general than in detail. We cannot even make mention of the names of the vigorous, progressive, practical men who have been active and prominent in making the history of the town; nor of the power behind the throne, the good women of Columbus, each a queen in her own realm. And we must pass by with a mere mention the banquet tendered by the Columbus Commercial Club, a generous and appetizing spread, graced by beauty, wit and intelligence, and enlivened by a "feast of reason and a flow of soul." Summarized, Columbus, from our view, is a community of good mannered and well behaved people, energetic, very hospitable, up-to-date, who have learned the accurate measurement of their physical, mental and nervous forces, and how to apply them correctly in the surest way to secure the best results. A people who, caring well for themselves, are able and always ready to offer to any strangers who may come within their gates, seeking good homes or safe opportunities for investment, facilities and inducements that are equalled by few and surpassed by fewer cities in the state of Indiana, or anywhere in all the great west. In a word and in final, a people who can say for themselves and who can show to others that...

For him, who has the nerve to try.
Some means of some kind may be found,
To climb the rock, however high,
Or to open up a way around.

Impressions of Brother Remy
The Republic. December 12, 1901 p. 2
What He Saw During His Recent Visit to Our Little City. The Schools and Churches. The Many Sound Industrial Institutions Are Written in a Pleasing Style by the Seymour Republican Editor.

E. A. Remy, of the *Seymour Republican*, gleaned considerable information regarding Columbus' many factories and institutions and has put them in the shape of a neat write up which appeared in his paper recently. He says:

The recent visit of the Southern Indiana Press Association to Columbus furnished an opportunity for a goodly company of keenly observant men and women to see one of the very best cities in the Hoosier state, and to enjoy the hospitality of a generous people. The visitors were given a royal welcome and for, twenty-four hours they practically owned the center of population city. Columbus is a city of beautiful homes, fine churches, superior schools, a splendid public library, commodious public buildings, clean streets, nearly fifty miles of cement sidewalks, and manufacturing industries employing 1,600 men. The city owns its water and light plants and supports a paid fire department. The affairs of the city are economically administered, the tax levy being 85 cents for all purposes on an assessed valuation of property of $5,000,000. And within her population Columbus has numerous enterprising public spirited men who are investing capital and conducting business enterprises that furnish employment to a large number of men.

MANUFACTORIES

Columbus has cause to be proud of her manufactories. Most of these plants were visited by the newspaper party, and what was observed as a revelation to the visitors, likewise to Columbus people who had never before taken the time to ascertain what their home factories were doing. The Orinoco Tannery Company is one of the newer industries there, having been organized about five years ago, by Columbus men. It employs about fifty men and the business done the past year amounts to about 3225, 000. The Orinoco Furniture Factory produces as high a grade of furniture ad manufactured any place. Their principal line is parlor tables, of which they manufacture a number of styles. The plant is finely equipped and employs about 100 men. This factory's product has wide reputation for its excellence. The Columbus Hand and Tool Company is one of the best and most prosperous plants of its kind in the west, and has been in successful operation for a dozen years or more, and employs a large force of men. Glanton's Furniture Factory, owned by James Glanton, manufactures hall trees exclusively, and is doing high grade work, giving employment to a big force of skilled workmen at good wages. The Reeves Pulley Company was incorporated in 1888, and has since manufactured wood split pulleys on a large scale. The plant has grown from a rather small beginning to one of large proportions employing 200 men. Besides the manufacture of pulleys in this factory is also manufactured the Reeves Variable Speed Transmission, which has developed into a large business itself. This factory's product is marketed all over the world.

Reeves & Company manufacture threshing machinery and saw mills, their factory being the largest in Columbus. The plant covers several acres of ground and the main building is three stories high. Here from 300 to 500 men are employed, building a grade of machinery that brings the top price. The gross sales of Reeves & Company in 1900 exceeded one and one-quarter million dollars, and the indications point to even a larger business in 1902. This is, indeed, a great plant. The Mooney Tannery is the largest manufacturer of hand-stuffed oak tanned leather in the United States. The product of his tannery represents the highest attainment in the tanner's art. There is no better leather than that which comes from the Mooney tannery. This plant employs from 150 to 200 men.

Besides these there is the National Machine Company, Columbus Saddlery Company, two large planing mills, and other smaller enterprises. It is the pride of the Columbus factories that they put out nothing shoddy or cheap. With these industrial plants all in successful operation and with all her other advantages, Columbus is prosperous and has a bright future. Her people are happy and loyal to their city, as they ought to be. Then surrounded as Columbus is with as fine farming land as there is in the state, with the famous Hawpatch and the rich valley of White River to draw from, she will get a trade that will always be worth hundreds of thousands annually. In short there is only one better and more promising city in Southern Indiana than Columbus, and that is Seymour, our own home, but we will always have a good word for our hospitable neighbor on the north.

The Hopper
The Republic. February 17, 1902 p. 4
S. B. Beasecker, who resigned as manager of the Columbus Saddlery Co. some time ago, and went with his family to Sheboygan, has returned to Columbus and has taken a position with the Mooney tannery as traveling salesman. It is understood that he will move his family back to this city.

The Hopper
The Republic. April 7, 1902 p. 4
F. M. Harvey, a currier at the Mooney tannery, is a candidate for city marshal on the Republican ticket, as will be seen in the announcement column. Mr. Harvey is a laboring man, a staunch Republican and possesses all the qualifications for the office.

Looking For Her Husband
The Republic. April 18, 1902 p. 4
Mrs. Charles Apel Says He Left Here the Latter Part of August.

Mrs. Charles Apel, who lives with her mother Mrs. Sarah Jacobs, Twelfth and Union streets, is looking for her husband, who, she says, deserted her the latter part of August, leaving on the excursion to Benton Harbor. She says she thinks he is either in Columbus now, or in Indianapolis.

She says that on the day before the excursion he beat her eldest daughter, Lottie Wink, aged eight years. Mrs. Apel says she was married to Apel two years ago and that she was a widow at that time, being left with two children. At the time he deserted her they were living at Tenth and Union, where she continued to keep house until recently. Mr. Apel is a carpenter and was formerly employed at Mooney's tannery.

Council Elect Fills Offices
The Republic. April 18, 1902 p. 8
Police Force Strong Morally and Physically is Named. Much Care in Selecting. Caucus Held in the Office of John W. Morgan Lasting From Early in the Evening Until Midnight — The Officers.

Tuesday evening the newly elected mayor and council held a caucus in the office of John W. Morgan, Fourth and Washington streets, for the purpose of filling the appointive offices. The business was carefully conducted, and the only trouble seemed to be a selection from the many good names under consideration, and the meeting lasted until midnight. [...]

The council-elect certainly could not have made better appointments than it did Tuesday evening. All who were chosen are upright, moral and conscientious citizens. The appointment of the police is an especially commendable transaction. Newton Clark is a sober, industrious man and will make an excellent officer. For the last five years he has been employed at the Mooney tannery. He lives in the first ward. [...]

Terminal Will Be Built Here

The Republic. July 16, 1902 p. 5

Few Realize What an Excellent Thing the Electric Line Is. Will Have Large Pay Roll. Interview With Will G. Irwin Regarding the Proposed Extension of the Inter-urban Line to This City.

While it is generally conceded that the proposed extension of the Indianapolis, Greenwood & Franklin electric line from Franklin to this city would be a benefit to our people, very few persons are aware of the fact that if the Messrs. Irwin secure the required franchises this city would be made the terminal of the road. That means the building of a car barn, repair shops, station and other departments necessary to conduct the business. Will G. Irwin was seen by Republican news writer this morning and courteously gave out some very interesting facts regarding the proposed extension. [...]

The terminal will be an institution that will be of far more value than any industrial institution here excepting the Mooney tannery, Reeves & Co.'s plant and the Reeves Pulley works.

Personal Points
The Republic. August 16, 1902 p. 5
Fred Wetzel, traveling salesman for Mooney's tannery, returned home last evening from Anderson.

Sherman McKay
The Republic. September 9, 1902 p. 5
Sherman McKay, aged twenty-eight years, died Monday midnight of consumption, at the home of his father, Isaac McKay, 1327 Union street. Mr. McKay was an employee at the Mooney Tannery and had many friends who sympathize with the bereaved relatives. Funeral services will be held Wednesday morning at 9 o'clock at the residence, conducted by Rev. F. O. Lamoreux. Burial will be made in Liberty graveyard.

Mangled Body Found on Track
The Republic. October 29, 1902 p. 5
John Mitchell, a Well Known Electrician, Meets Death. Entire Family Ill-fated. Two Brothers and Nephew Met Deaths and John Was Victim to Seemingly Interminable Chain of Accidents.

John Mitchell, a well-known and popular resident of this city, was found dead on the Pennsylvania tracks in this city Tuesday night about 9 o'clock. From all evidence possible to glean, Mitchell was either violently struck or ran over by a train. [...]

William Mitchell was another brother who met an untimely death. Nine years ago, while employed at the Mooney tannery, a barrel of tallow fell on him with fatal results.

Both Sides of Trust, Tariff, Reciprocity and Expansion

The Republic. November 1, 1902 p. 5
One of the Most Important and Brilliant Speeches Ever Heard in Bartholomew Delivered by Beveridge. Speaker Paid Deserved Compliment to Miller. Trusts are the Natural Outcome of a Wonderful Advance in Industry and Enormous Increase in Population — Slanderous Outrage Perpetrated on the Nation by the Opposition Party — Question Now is Where Shall We Find New Markets.

The speech delivered by Senator A. J. Beveridge Friday evening was undoubtedly one of the greatest ever heard at a political campaign in Bartholomew county. The discourse was a broad one, covering both sides of trusts, tariff, reciprocity and expansion, and Mr. Beveridge brought forth many important points that the ordinary person does does not think of. [...]

Suppose a wire connecting with Mooney's tannery should break. Business to some little extent would be crippled not only there but would spread out to the entire field covered by that institution. Just such little things as that circle out to the confines of the nation's industry. The battle of New Orleans was fought long after peace was declared. That was because communication was slow then. Now a message can be flashed around the entire globe in a few minutes. Eighty millions of people are now gathered together in a mutual, compact mass called the American nation, and nothing but organized industry, such as the railroad, the telephones, etc., could serve the people.

Clarance O. Sweany Killed at Tannery
The Republic. March 28, 1903 p. 5
After the paper went to press it is learned at 4 o'clock that Clarence O. Sweany, a tanner employed at the Mooney tannery, was killed by being caught in a pulley. The fatal accident occurred shortly before 4 o'clock. The remains were taken to Davidson & Henderson's establishment. Sweany lived at 1527 Union street.

Fatal Accident Befell Sweany
The Republic. March 28, 1903 p. 5
No One Was Near When He Was Caught on the Shaft. Unconscious When Removed — Remains Taken to Seymour for Burial, Accompanied by a Large Party of Friends — Was a Member of the Maccabees.

The remains of Clarence O. Sweany, the young man who accidentally met death Saturday afternoon at W. W. Mooney & Sons' tannery, were taken Sunday evening to Seymour Funeral services were conducted at 3 o'clock this afternoon at the home of his mother, Mrs. Jennie Ross, and the body was laid to rest in a country graveyard near Seymour. About 4:30 o'clock Sunday evening the remains were taken from Davidson & Hendersons's establishment, where they had rested since Saturday evening, and were accompanied by a very large gathering of friends to the train which leaves here shortly after 5 o'clock. The following fellow workmen, all members of Columbus Tent, No. 137, Knights of the Maccabees, acted as pall bearers: John Weiler, Fred Wetzel, Bert McMillan, Joseph Miller, Daniel Greenfield, Richard Bearhope, Augustus E. Walford and George P. Herndon. About fifty Knights of the Maccabees accompanied the remains to Seymour, most of them returning on the late train Sunday night. The following well-known men composed the party:

John Troutman, Smith W. Snively, John T. Fellows, Robert M. Henry, John Stevens, Alva Herndon, George W. Carter, John Cooper, George Bearhope, Richard Bearhope, George P. Herndon, John G. Weiler, Amos Bolinger, Joseph Hingston, Samuel J. Wetzel, W. H. Kyte, William Smith, Ed Horton, Frank Kennard, George Smiths, Alexander Sallivan, Carl Van Wye, James Miller, Frank Hill, James Olmstead, John Lune, Jesse Davis, John Sertz, Frank Harris, William Young, Fred Wetzel, Joseph Smith, Stephen Hall, Guy Kelley, Daniel Greenfield, Bert McMillan, Augustus E. Walford, Albert Gilmore, J. J. Lash,

A. K. McCloskey, Bert Snively, Peter Lambert, William Pruitt and R. E. Wagner.

The Fatal Accident
Facts other than that he was killed by being whirled around a shaft cannot be secured. No one was near when he was caught, and besides the place where he met his death is an out of the way part of the building. What prompted him to get near this particular shaft, or how he was caught, cannot be explained. The accident occurred in the leach house, which is a building at the north end of the tannery. Sweany and William Vaughn were engaged that afternoon pitching leaches, or to be more plain, emptying tanks of tan bark by shoveling the contents through a hole in the bottom, where the bark is caught up and carried away by a drag chain. Two men are usually put at this work and they work alternately a few minutes at a time. While one is working the other is at ease. About 8 o'clock Sweany got out of the tank and left his fellow workman, presumably to watch the drag chain lest it choke up with the tan bark, which is often the case. Sweany had left the tank only three or four minutes when Mr. Vaughn and John Noblitt, the foreman of the leach house, heard a strange noise at the south end of the building. Mr. Noblitt hurried there to ascertain the trouble only to be confronted with the horrible sight of a tangled mass of humanity being wound around a shaft. Mr. Vaughn was on the scene, too, in an instant. Mr. Noblitt hurried to the engine room and had the machinery stopped, when he

and Mr. Vaughn took the almost lifeless body from the shaft. At that time Sweany was unconscious and lived only a few minutes.

Peculiar Occurrence

The shaft on which Sweany was caught is about $2\frac{3}{16}$ inches in diameter, and revolves at the comparatively slow rate of about sixty to sixty-five revolutions a minute. It is not an extraordinary thing for workmen to come into close contact with shafts, and besides, there is no set screw on which Sweany's clothing could have caught. When found the young man's right arm was hooked over the shaft and was broken in several places. Other bones were fractured and his body was considerably mangled and bruised. His work did not take him to that part of the building, and it is seldom that any of the work men have business there. All these facts go to make the occurrence a strange one.

Clarence O. Sweany was born in Jackson county and was twenty-one years, three months and one day old. At the age of about seventeen he left Jackson county and went to Tennessee, from which state he came to this city two years ago. Ever since that time he worked at the Mooney tannery. He was classed among the most faithful workmen and was very poplar among his follow employees.

Was a Maccabee

Last December he joined Columbus Tent, No. 137, K. O. T. M., together with a class of about forty people. He took out a $500 policy which he intended giving his mother for a Christmas present. There was some error which caused a delay and the young man was much disappointed in not being able to make the present to his mother until some time after that holiday.

The Hopper
The Republic. March 4, 1903 p. 8
Mrs. Charles A. Ross, mother of Clarence O. Sweany, who was killed in Mooney's tannery last Saturday, is in the city to day to attend to matters with regard to the policy held by the unfortunate young man.

Suit for Divorce
The Republic. July 10, 1903 p. 8
The following suit has been filed in the Circuit Court: Rade M. Nelson vs. Albert J. Nelson, for divorce and custody of child. Failure to provide is alleged in the complaint. Mrs. Nelson is a stenographer at Money's tannery. W. J. Beck attorney for the plaintiff.

New Roth Pitless Pump
The Republic. October 30, 1903 p. 10
Given Test Yesterday Afternoon — Shown To Be a Wonder in Number of Ways.

A test was given the Roth Pitless pump this afternoon at a well located on the Mooney tannery lot, and proved a wonder to a number of visitors. The pump is the invention of J. G. Roth, of this city, and is intended to pump water for irrigating rice lands. A number of the pumps are already in successful operation to the south, taking the place of pumps that have to be located in a pit close to the surface water. This is rotary pump and has a capacity, according to size and speed, of from 500 to 2,000 gallons per minute.

The test was witnessed by J. K Sharp, Jr., F. L. Sattle, of Indianapolis, H. M. Campbell, B. M. Boyd, M. O. Reeves, W. H. N. Haggard, Harry Schowe, M. T. Reeves, E. Olay, H. H. Bassett and others, and is pronounced a great success by persons knowing something about pumps.

Great Damage Done by High Water
The Republic. March 26, 1904 p. 5
Great Damage Done by High Water. Near Mark Reached Six Years Ago the Whole County is Affected by the Hardest Rainfall Known in This Country for the Past Several Years — Damage to Crops.

Although the damage to property has not been reported to be so great the water is as high as it was in the flood of 1898. All day long reports have been coming in from different parts of the county making the story more disastrous to property owners and the county in general. The flood has been hard to handle, hard because it covered so much territory and hard because so many people had different stories of the same happenings. [...]

Money's tannery closed down this morning as the water came into the lower part of the tannery and almost submerged the hair house. Happy Hollow was deserted this morning and a trip to that part of the city showed that nearly all of the residents had either moved or were moving.

Case Was Long on Court Docket
The Republic. April 30, 1904 p. 8
Case Was Long on Court Docket. Pennsylvania Lines Vs. Mooney Lateral Railway Company. Filed Twenty Years Ago.

A case that has been on the docket for over twenty years was dismissed this morning at the cost of the plaintiff. This was the suit of the Pennsylvania lines against the Mooney Lateral Railway Company, for an injunction. The Mooney company was incorporated to build a short line connected the Mooney tannery with the Big Four line so that cars could be loaded at the plant. The track of the Lateral company had to cross the Pennsylvania tracks and the latter company sued for an injunction against Mooneys. The case had been pending in court ever since filed and although it has been called up repeatedly nothing was ever done. The number of the case was 2,119 and the last case filed is 4,887, showing that over 2,000 cases have been filed since the action brought by the railroad company. [...]

May Effect Combination
The Republic. May 11, 1904 p. 5
Talk of League Base Ball Team Composed of Tannery and Post Office Employees.

There is some talk of a combination between the post office and Money's tannery in order to furnish the material for a first class baseball team. It is the understanding that Saturday half holidays will be instituted at the tannery and this will give the baseball enthusiasts of that plant a chance to work out. The matter of the combination will be taken up to-night by the managers of the respective leagues and some disposition made of it. The post office team is said to be a strong one but there are hardly enough available men to select a first class baseball team. Great preparations are being made for the game Saturday and either Starkey or Schoonover will pitch the game. As soon as MacCaffey gets in shape he will do box duty for the government officials.

Was Robbed of Money
The Republic. July 15, 1904 p. 1
Chas. Lefler Has His Pockets Rifled While Asleep Near An Open Window.

Charles Lefter, who lives on north Jackson street and who is employed as an engineer at the Mooney tannery, was robbed last night of $13. The robbery has been reported to the authorities and they are at work on it but there is no clue to follow.

Mr. Lefler was sleeping near an open window and had thrown his trousers, containing the money, over a chair. The chair was but short distance from the window and he thinks that the robbers simply reached in and secured the trousers, going through them and then putting them back on the chair. In his opinion no one entered the house.

In Society's Domain
The Republic. October 1, 1904 p. 8
Golden Wedding

In response to cordial invitations which were extended several weeks ago about 300 relatives and friends gathered at the home of Mr. and Mrs. John Schinnerer, west of the city, yesterday in celebration of their golden wedding anniversary. From 11 o'clock until 4 o'clock an elaborate course dinner was served. Everyone enjoyed the day and the host and hostess, who requested that no presents be sent, received not only the hearty congratulations from their friends but many beautiful and costly presents.

John Schinnerer, who was the son of John Orban and Eva Schinnerer, was born in Windsheim, Bavaria, Germany, November 11, 1833, where he was educated, and following in the footsteps of his father became a cooper. Fifty years ago, at the age twenty-one, he was married at Frankfort-on-the-Main to Sarah Brandt, who was born in Baden in 1831. They set sail tor America in the fall of 1854 and arriving in New York City went to Troy, where they lived for two years when they came to Indiana and located in this city, and twenty-five years ago moved to their farm west of the city where they now reside. While engaged in the cooper trade Mr. Schinnerer made all of the vats for Money's Tannery. To them were born eleven children, seven of whom are dead. The living are Mrs. Matilda Miller, of Indianapolis; Christian, of Ottawa, Kan.; Mrs. Julia Aickle, of Indianapolis and Henrietta Swanke, of this county.

Mr. Schinnerer's life on the farm has been an exceptionally prosperous one and by the aid of his estimable wife he has, by thrift and good management, acquired a great fortune.

The Hopper
The Republic. January 31, 1905 p. 8
Roy Jones, who is employed at the Mooney Tannery, suffering from the effects of burns about the head and face. He tried to start a fire with coal oil and the blaze enveloped his face. His hair was singed and his eyebrows burned off.

Fight at the Tannery
The Republic. February 1, 1905 p. 5
Charles Garrett and George Burk in a Mix up in which Both are Cut Up Some.

Charles Garrett and George Burk, both employees of the Mooney Tannery, were cut and bruised this afternoon in a fight. Garrett was the worse injured of the two, and was badly cut about the head and neck. Bark received an ugly gash on the head, but after he had been taken to a physician he was able to return to work.

The story of the fight was hard to get, as each participant did not care to talk. Burk was taken to the office of Dr. J. W. Arnold, where he said a door had fallen on him and injured him. A short time after Garrett was takes to the office of Dr. Wood, and it was learned that the two had been in a fight. Bark then admitted having been in a scrap, and claimed that Garrett was the aggressor.

Burk says that he and Garrett were working together, when Garrett told him if he did not work faster he would "take a bat at him." Burk says he informed Garrett he could bat away and the fight then started. It seems that both had knives, as both were out. Marshal Horton is investigating the care.

Garrett was seen at the office of Dr. Wood this afternoon and said the trouble was caused by an old grudge. He claims that Burk came at him with a trimming knife and cut him on the chin. He claims to have only struck Burk with his fist but gashes on Bark's head seem to dispute this statement. Garrett is cut on the right hand and back of the left ear, besides being cut on the chin. He and Burk roomed together for about two weeks and then Burk secured other lodgings. Both will probably be arrested and given a chance to explain the trouble in court.

Injured on Elevator
The Republic. March 1, 1905 p. 1

John Shroyer Fell from Fourth Floor of Mooney Tannery to Bottom — Thirty Feet.

John Shroyer, aged about thirty years, was badly injured at the tannery of W. W. Mooney Sons, Wednesday morning about 9 o'clock. He is now confined to his bed at his home on Sycamore street, near the railroad crossing.

Shroyer was on the freight elevator with a roll of leather and in some manner the elevator dropped from the fourth floor to the bottom, distance of about thirty feet. No bones were broken but Shroyer was badly bruised and injured. Dr. J. W. Benham was called and attended the injured man.

Dr. Benham says it will be few days before he can determine whether or not Shroyer is injured internally.

The Hopper
The Republic. March 8, 1905 p. 8

Yesterday afternoon John Hofer, of the American Express Company, delivered a package at the office of the Mooney Tannery. Near the tannery is an abandoned well which is boarded over. The horse hitched to the express wagon fell in this well and was terribly scalded by escaping steam, one of the steam pipes having been directed into the well on account of its being used for no other purpose. The horse was finally pulled out and is not expected to recover from the accident.

The Hopper
The Republic. March 21, 1905 p. 8

The *Indianapolis News* last night contained dispatch purporting to be from Nashville which stated that Joseph Hingston, a young man who had lately come to this city from Ireland, had, after long search, found his sweetheart and it was the supposition that they could be married soon and live happily ever after. The facts in the case are that the Hingston named is a resident of this city. He did come from Ireland some time ago but he did not come in search of his sweetheart. He is a cousin of the Rev. G. D. Wolfe and is employed in the Mooney tannery. The dispatch was a fake from the date line to the last word, the girl in the story never having existed. It seems a pity that the correspondent, whoever it was, should leave his native county and impose his stories on Columbus people. It would evidently be better if he would stay at home where he has more raw material with which to work.

Why So Timid?
The Republic. May 19, 1905 p. 4

The following appears in the *Times*: "One of the afternoon papers contained an article about an enlargement of and extensive improvements to be added to the Mooney Tannery plant. W. A. Mooney stated, when asked concerning the matter, that he could make no statement except to say that the whole story was a lie."

Why don't the *Times* state where the above appeared and not be so timid. The *Herald* is the afternoon paper referred to and it seems strange that the *Times* hesitates to speak out, it was not so bashful formerly.

Wants, For Sale, Etc.
The Republic. May 19, 1905 p. 5
LOST - Small coin purse, between Wolf's meat market and Hammond's restaurant. Return to Mrs. Nelson, at Mooney's tannery office, and get reward.

Assessments Show Increase in County
The Republic. June 23, 1905 p. 1
The statement of the assessments of the different corporations in Columbus and Bartholomew county given out by the board of review shows a gain in the county over last year of $179,622.09 for the present year. This is in the face of reductions made in some local corporations. The totals do not include the telephone lines, railroads, interurban roads, telegraph lines and express companies doing business in the county, these corporations being assessed by the state board of tax commissioners. [...]

There is a decrease in the assessment of Reeves & Company and an increase in the Mooney Tannery, it not being assessed as a corporation last year.

Deputy E. E. Earl Makes a Big Haul

The Republic. July 11, 1905 p. 1

When Addison Wayt, George Wayt and William West pleaded guilty in Justice Stader court this morning to violations of the fish law one of the biggest hauls in the county was recorded. The total fines and costs in the three cases amounted to $243, and but one of the fines has been paid.

The three men were charged with using dynamite to kill the fish when the affidavits were filed by Deputy Fish Commissioner E. E. Earl, yesterday, but this morning when the three men were brought into court it was found that the state would be unable to prove that dynamite was used. The state had evidence, however, that the men had stretched a seine across White river near Azalia, and had then thrown some kind of an explosive into the river which killed the fish. It was the plan to let the dead fish float down to the seine where they would be caught.

When the three men were charged with using a seine each pleaded guilty, and a plea of guilty was also entered to the charge of using an explosive substance which either killed or stupified the fish so they could be caught easily. Each man was fined $40.50, and the costs in each case amounted to $40.50, making each fine and cost $81. Addison Wayt paid his fine and cost and stayed the fines of George Wayt and William West. The latter is a young man who lives in this city and who is employed at the Mooney Tannery.

Deputy Commissioner Earl said this morning that these three cases were all he had to make public at this time, but he intimated that there would be more to follow. He has information to the effect that there have been numerous flagrant violations of the fish law in this county, and there are plenty of deputies in the county on the lookout for violators.

The Hopper
The Republic. July 21, 1905 p. 8
A telephone message came from Alpha Mitchell, of Shelbyville, Wednesday, stated that his brother, Carl, had been killed at Columbus. Mrs. Mitchell and daughter went up on the afternoon train and found her boy working like a "trooper" at Mooney's tannery. — *North Vernon Sun.*

The Hopper
The Republic. August 3, 1905 p. 8
John Lister had a very narrow escape from being mashed by the cave-in of a sewer near the Mooney tannery yesterday. He was employed by Stillinger & Lee, who were digging a sewer near the tannery, and at a weak place in the bank the dirt and tan bank caved in. A mortar bed started over the brink but the men grabbed it in time to save Lister. A quantity of tan bark and dirt fell on him, but by quick work he was pulled out before suffering any injury.

The Hopper
The Republic. October 24, 1905 p. 8

Some of the friends of a young Kentuckian who is a member of the office staff at Mooney's tannery perpetrated a practical joke on him a few days ago. The young man was slightly indisposed and being almost an entire stranger in the city he asked his friends to direct him to a good doctor. His friends very promptly, but blandly, directed him to Dr. Dryden, in the office of whom he waited some time for the return of the doctor who was temporarily absent, only to be informed on his return that the doctor was a veterinary surgeon.

The Hopper
The Republic. November 16, 1905 p. 8

Hege & Company is finishing up the work on the new addition to the Mooney tannery. The roof is being put on and all of the work will be completed soon.

The Hopper
The Republic. November 21, 1905 p. 8

Elder William H. Book of the Tabernacle, preached to the employees of the Mooney tannery at noon to-day and he reports a large audience and an interesting service.

An East Columbus Fire
The Republic. December 21, 1905 p. 2
In the Home of Edward Miller has the Appearance of Being Work of Incendiary.

A fire, the origin of which is somewhat of a mystery, occurred in the home of Edward Miller, on the "Nigger Hill" road, in East Columbus, at 9:30 o'clock Wednesday night. At 9 o'clock Wednesday morning Mrs. Miller went to the home of her neighbor, Mrs. John Wagner, where she remained until the fire occurred. She left no fire in her home, nor did any member of the Miller family enter the household from the time that Mrs. Miller left it until the fire occurred. Mr. Miller, who is employed at Money's tannery, went to his work early Wednesday morning, nor did he return until he was informed that his house was on fire Wednesday night.

The fire started in the sitting room of the building and damaged the room and furniture to a considerable extent before it was extinguished by the volunteer bucket brigade of East Columbus. The building was insured for $500.

The circumstances surrounding the fire seem to indicate that it was of incendiary origin.

Dinner
The Republic. January 1, 1906 p. 5
George H. Lucas gave a dinner at Hammond's Cafe last night in honor of Brown Mantel, who will go on the road for the Mooney tannery. The table was decorated with cut flowers, and covers were laid for

Miss Louise Keye, Miss Ruby Campbell, Miss Addie Smith, of Hartford City, Mr. Harry Bevis, Mr. Mantel and Mr. Lucas.

At the Churches
The Republic. January 27, 1906 p. 5
Tabernacle Christian [...] on Tuesday, at the noon hour, preaching at Mooney's tannery. Friday, at the noon hour, at Reeves Company. A cordial welcome to all of these meetings.

The Hopper
The Republic. January 30, 1906 p. 8
Brown Mantel, who has been a member of the office force of the Mooney tannery for some time, left this morning for his first trip on the road in the interests of the company.

Prospectus is Issued
The Republic. February 10, 1906 p. 5
Louisville & Indianapolis Traction Company Says Nice Things About Columbus.

The Louisville & Indianapolis Traction Company has issued a prospectus showing the country through which the line will run when connection is completed from Louisville to Indianapolis by way of Columbus.

The prospectus gives excellent pictures of the Mooney tannery and both the foundry and main factory buildings of Reeves & Company. There is an extensive story about Columbus and its industries and the town is given a good send off. Other towns and cities along the line are also featured, a street scene in Franklin being shown. There is a relief map showing the hills and "mountains" through and over which the road will pass and on the map the road runs on the west side of the river. The Irwins have not yet decided which side of the river will be used but most people believe the line will finally be built on the west side.

The Hopper
The Republic. February 13, 1906 p. 8
The Rev. Charles Gorman Richards will have charge of the Bible study at the Tabernacle to-night at 7:30 o'clock and will give an exposition on the fifteenth chapter of St. Mark. This meeting is usually conducted by the Rev. W. H. Book and Rev. Richards takes charge of it to-night on account of the death of Mrs. Book. Rev. Richards also spoke in place of Rev. Book at the Mooney tannery to-day.

The Hopper
The Republic. February 19, 1906 p. 8
The police of Seymour arrested a young man in that city Friday night on charge of having burglarized W. H. Reynolds grocery store. The prisoner confessed to the charge, and in default $500 bond he was taken to the county jail in Brownstown to await the action of the grand jury. The prisoner gave his name as Elmer Haycock and said that he had formerly been employed at a tannery in Columbus, but nothing is known of him at Mooney's tannery in this city.

Great Increase in Local Freight

The Republic. March 14, 1906 p. 1

Pennsylvania Officials Do Not Know Where the Finish Will Be. Cars Are In Demand. Columbus Manufacturers are Heavy Shippers and the Freight from this City Goes to all Parts of the Country.

Few people here realize how much business Columbus is doing and how good the town is, said an official of the Pennsylvania lines this morning as he looked over pile after pile of freight in the local freight house. Drays were coming and going, freight was being received and sent away and a corps of clerks were busy with bills, invoices and the like. In the yards the switch engine was coughing at the weather while it yanked box cars here and there to be used perhaps by local people or to be unloaded for local business men.

For the past five years there has been a steady increase in the freight business of the Pennsylvania lines at Columbus. The officials have wondered where the limit could be and they are still wondering, because the increase keeps right on. There is enough more business being done this year than there was last and it keeps right on. What the local official said about how little the people realized the magnitude of the business done here is literally true. Twelve or fifteen cars have been placed within the past two days for the use of Columbus men. The cars go to the grain dealers, to the Mooney tannery, the Reeves factories, local builders, the Iron Works and other places. The demand for cars is almost too great to supply but as this is a junction point the manufacturers here are taken better care of than if they happened to be in Madison, Seymour or some other point on the road. These cars have been placed with people who are shipping products to points all over the country. [...]

Great Increase in Local Freight
The Republic. March 14, 1906 p. 1
Lowlands Covered by the Big River. Crump Levee Went Out Last Night, Giving River More Sway. Golf Links Under Water. Family Living in Club House Forced to Get a Boat and Move Out-mail Carriers Are Unable to Deliver Their Mall.

Although it was thought that White river had reached a stand Tuesday afternoon, water from some source or other started the river on another boom last night and it raised about eighteen inches during the night. This morning it was still slowly raising but Engineer Rush, at the water works, thought it would stand this afternoon. Hawcreek has fallen perceptibly and at Clifford it was stated this morning that Flatrock was falling. At Edinburg there is a big river and it was reported from there that the water was within a few inches of the danger mark. [...]

The golf links were flooded last night and Newton Sanders, who has been making his home in the club house, had to get a boat and move out to-day. Some of the people in Happy Hollow also had to move and in a few instances neighbors were visiting each other in boats to-day. The Blackwood mill was not running to-day, as the first floor is covered with water and the river is almost surrounding the building. The high water also crept to within striking distance of the Mooney tannery this morning and the low lands near the Driving Park were flooded.

Fund is Still Growing
The Republic. April 28, 1906 p. 8
Fourteen Hundred Reached by the Fund which Local People are Raising.

The fund which Columbus people are raising for the benefit of the California sufferers continues to grow and Hugh Th. Miller, treasurer of the general committee, reported this afternoon that $1,400.42 had been either paid or pledged. Another remittance was made by Mr. Miller to-day which makes a total of $1,000 sent away to the proper authorities.

Mooney's tannery, including the office force, has raised $100 and paid it into the treasury of the general committee and the Columbus Street Railway & Light Company has donated $20.75. The Women's Relief Corps has contributed $5. From other organizations $361.34 have been sent away.

City Safe Again
The Republic. August 20, 1906 p. 5
The city of Columbus again has water and fire protection after having been without either for practically thirty hours. The old pump was not started until about five o'clock Sunday afternoon, and the water

did not get up town until about twenty minutes after that time.

The efforts of the men at the water works were directed most all day Saturday to some way in which the old pump could be primed but late in the afternoon this task was given up as impossible and the work of making the repairs on the broken new pump was pushed forward. About ten o'clock the new wrist pin was fitted into place and everything was in readiness when the officials found the problem of how to start the new pump confronting them. All efforts to fill the pump with enough water to prime it failed. George Herndon, engineer at the Mooney tannery, offered his services and started the pumps at the tannery in the effort to pump enough water into the new pump to prime it. The main at Fifth and Brown streets was shut off so that all of this water would come into the new pump. The Mooney pumps were kept going most of the night, and about four o'clock Sunday morning there was almost enough water to prime with, but at that time the wells at the tannery went dry and all of the night's work went for nothing. [...]

The Hopper
The Republic. September 4, 1906 p. 8
Edgar Abbott has resigned his position as salesman at the Hub shoe store, and has accepted a place at the Mooney tannery.

An Abandoned Factory

The Republic. September 21, 1906 p. 4

Brush Block and Heel Stock Factory on Fourth Street Moving to Ashtabula, O.

The brush block and heel stock factory owned by Thomas F. Robinson and for the past several years operated by him at the west end of Fourth street has gone out of business so far as Columbus is concerned and the plant is being moved to Ashtabula, Ohio. Mr. Robinson will follow with his family next week and will reengage in the manufacture of brush block and heel stock at Ashtabula.

It became necessary for Mr. Robinson to abandon the business in this city because machinery for shaving leather has been installed at the Mooney tannery. Before the machinery was installed at the tannery the leather was shaved by hand and the shavings thus procured were suitable for the manufacture of brush blocks and heel stocks, whereas the shavings obtained from the machines are unfit for that purpose. Mr. Robinson says that since locating in Columbus he has done quite well from a standpoint of business and that he is leaving the city from necessity and not from choice.

The Hopper

The Republic. September 22, 1906 p. 8

Jacob Bosswell, an employee at Mooney's tannery, was accidentally struck on the abdomen by a piece of machinery while at work this morning and for a time appeared to be dangerously injured. He was removed to his home on north Mechanic street and on the way to his home he was taken to Dr. John Little Morris, who pronounced his injury not of a serious nature.

Sustained Broken Arm
The Republic. October 20, 1906 p. 1
Henry Schoonover, Jr., son of Councilman Schoonover, who was working at Mooney's tannery, sustained a broken arm this morning while working in the line of his duties at the tannery. The young man's arm was caught between a rope and a shaft and the bones of the forearm were crushed and broken before he could be rescued from his perilous position by his fellow workmen. The injured man was taken to the office of Dr. Banker, where the fracture was reduced by Drs. Weamer and A. J. Banker.

Wire Clothes Line Proves Death Trap
The Republic. November 21, 1906 p. 1
Busy Season Gives a Brighter Outlook. Columbus Has Had Prosperous Year — Better One is Coming. Review of Conditions.

[...] A comparatively new industry in Columbus is the hoop factory on north Washington street and while but little is said in print about this enterprise it has rapidly grown to be one of the most important in the city. It runs full time, employs a large number of men and is thriving in every way. The Mooney tannery has been doing a record breaking business this year and more business is in sight for next year.

The canning factory had a good season during the present year and some additions will likely be made there during the coming season. The Columbus Handle & Tool Company has had a busy year and is still hard at work. This is another company from which the people hear but little but nevertheless it has been running full time and sending its products everywhere handles and the like are used. The Caldwell & Drake Iron Works never had a better season than the present one. The plant runs until nine o'clock each night and the business has increased to such an extent that some new additions have been made and more are contemplated. It is the same story with the other factories and industries here, every department of business has been rushed to its fullest capacity and the outlook for the next year in every branch is even better than the outlook was this time last year. [...]

John Warner Falls Into His Wife's Arms
The Republic. January 2, 1907 p. 1
And Within a Few Minutes Expires of Organic Heart Disease At His Home on Fourth Street.

While in the act of lighting his pipe, preparatory to taking an after-breakfast smoke this morning John Warner, aged sixty years, fell into the arms of his wife and expired in a few moments. Death resulted from organic heart disease, from which he had long been a sufferer and from which he had been in a serious condition for the past three months.

The deceased formerly resided at Louisville, Ky.,

but came to Columbus one year ago and took employment in Mooney's tannery. His family joined him in Columbus last May. He leaves a wife and two children.

Attack of Smallpox May Result Fatality
The Republic. February 12, 1907 p. 1
After Eighteen Months Milton Walter's Smallpox Victim, Loses His Eyesight.

About one year and a half ago when there were a number of cases of smallpox in the neighborhood of First street in this city there were no fatalities from the contagion and most of the cases were inclined to be rather light attacks, yet at this late date it seems there is probability of a death as a result of the contagion.

At any rate Milton Walters is lying in a critical condition at his home at the corner of First and Brown streets and his condition is due to a case of smallpox that he contracted about eighteen months ago.

Walters recovered from the attack or at least it seemed that he had recovered and he returned to his work at Mooney's tannery. The disease settled in the patient's eyes and on his lungs and as a result of the affliction to his eyes he has become totally blind and the affliction to his lungs it is feared will cost him his life.

Small Boy Stabs a Drowsy Lodger

The Republic. February 13, 1907 p. 4

With a Butcher Knife in an Effort to Get Him Out of Bed and Succeeds — Deep Gash Inflicted.

While there are numerous methods of getting drowsy lodgers out of bed of mornings probably the most effective one was employed this morning, when a three-year-old son of George Hodler of Fourth street stuck a butcher knife into the arm of Charles Henry.

Henry, who is about eighteen years of age is employed at Mooney's tannery and boards at the Hodler home. The young man said he was not feeling well this morning and when called by a three-year-old son of his landlord he did not respond promptly. Again and again the little fellow attempted to induce the lodger to get up but without success and finally getting wholly out of patience with the drowsy lodger he seized a butcher knife and striking Henry on the right arm with it he inflicted a deep gash on the right arm, which Henry says will put him out of working commission for several days.

The Hopper

The Republic. March 7, 1907 p. 8

Sylvia Pittman, the young girl who was jailed by the police Tuesday night for the larceny of a pair of gold spectacles, was released from custody this afternoon. The board of childrens' guardians look up the girl's case but on learning her age they were obliged to abandon their effort in her behalf as her age placed her beyond the jurisdiction of the board. A cousin of the girl who is employed at Mooney's tannery had agreed to give her a good home and hence it was that the authorities decided to release her and give her another chance to be good.

The Hopper
The Republic. March 13, 1907 p. 8
Richard Bearhope, who has been in the office of the Mooney tannery here for some time has accepted a position as traveling salesman for the Mooney company. He left last night for Terre Haute, it being his first trip on the road.

The Hopper
The Republic. March 29, 1907 p. 8
Miss Blanche Smith, who has been connected with the Citizens Telephone Company for some time, has accepted a position as stenographer at the Mooney tannery and will begin her work there April 12.

Young Wife Leaves Her Home Suddenly
The Republic. April 5, 1907 p. 1
And With No Intimation to Her Husband of Her Intentions. She Kissed Him Goodbye. When He Left for His Work but When He Returned She Was Gone — Husband Searching for Her in Jackson County.

When Mrs. James Timbrook, of First street, kissed her husband goodbye before he went to his work at Money's tannery Wednesday morning as has been her custom since the couple's marriage on Dec. 15, he doubtless understood that the caress was sufficient unto the day only, but she evidently intended it to serve for all time, for when her husband returned in the evening from his work he learned that his wife had disappeared from her home, nor had she left any word of explanation regarding her sudden and unannounced departure.

When the husband returned from his work and found his wife of a few weeks absent he was not very greatly exercised over her absence as he supposed she was at the home of her sister. Mrs. Ed Truax, who resides in Orinoco, but later when she did not return he began an investigation, which resulted in his finding that when his wife left she took with her some of her clothing, some pictures and other mementos that are dear to the hearts of young wives. On making this discovery Mr. Timbrook went to the home of Mrs. Truax and not finding his wife there he boarded a train Thursday morning for Jackson county where his wife's people reside. Up to noon today no word had been received from the husband, nor had the absent wife returned.

Mrs. Timbrook was formerly Miss Edna Manuel and was, when married to James Timbrook a few weeks ago, twenty-two years of age. While her home was at Freetown, Jackson county, she had resided in Columbus for a considerable time before her marriage. The husband and his and her relatives in Columbus are at a loss to account for the young wife's strange conduct in leaving her home and husband without any explanation, for the couple are reported as having been getting along happily together and that the wife appeared perfectly contented with her matrimonial lot and her husband as well. The husband provided well for his wife and lavished on her and his home all the luxuries that his financial condition would permit.

She Promised Two But Married One
The Republic. April 8, 1907 p. 1
Miss Anna May Mudd Had Plenty of Excitement About Wedding. Mr. Johnson is Lucky His Engagement Had Been of Long, Standing and When He Found Another in the Way, He Hurriedly Married.

Ben Johnson and Miss Anna May Mudd, both colored, were married Saturday night between nine and ten o'clock by the Rev. Mr. Burtch, pastor of the Second Baptist church. The reason the hour of the marriage was rather late was because there was considerable excitement attending the proceedings.

According to the story told by the friends of the newly married couple Miss Mudd, who was employed as a domestic at the home of C. S. Way and. Mr. Johnson, who drives for Dr. A. J. Banker, had been engaged for some time. The date of the marriage had been named two or three times but every time it was postponed for some reason or other. The engagement was not broken but it was prolonged time and again and it is said that Miss Mudd grew weary of waiting.

At any rate Homer Paschell, a young colored man who works at the Mooney tannery, became attentive to Miss Mudd and it was whispered around that they were engaged. Saturday morning Mr. Paschell went to the office of County Clerk Godfrey and said he wanted to get a marriage license, he only wanted to fill out the application blank intended for himself and said Miss Anna May Mudd would be in later in the day and fill out her application blank. There was nothing unusual in this request so Clerk Godfrey filled out the blank for the man and laid It away until Miss Mudd should come in to fill out her application blank.

Nobody showed up during the day and Clerk Godfrey closed the office at the usual time in the evening. Saturday night about 7:30 o'clock the clerk received a hurry up call from Ben Johnson as the latter wanted to get a marriage license. Mr. Godfrey hastened to his office to accommodate Johnson and when he asked the name of the bride Mr. Johnson said the name was Anna May Mudd. The clerk was somewhat surprised at this be cause he knew there was part of an application already filled out for Miss Mudd and he did not see just how she was going to marry both Paschell and Johnson. Miss Mudd had accompanied Mr. Johnson, however, and she signed the application blank herself. The license was then issued and the couple routed out the Second Baptist minister who performed the ceremony.

Just what became of Mr. Paschell is not told but it is supposed that he got lost in the shuffle. The friends say that on Saturday morning Miss Mudd promised to marry Paschell and when he went to get the license without losing any time. In the meantime In the meantime Ben Johnson got word that his long engagement was about to be broken and that his sweetheart was going to marry another man. It was his time to get busy then and on account of his persuasive powers Miss Mudd agreed to marry him and left Mr. Mr. Paschell in the lurch, as the song says. As the situation now stands Mr. Paschell has half of a marriage license but Ben Johnson has a wife.

Shop Meetings
The Republic. April 8, 1907 p. 8
Shop meetings will be conducted by Evangelist Shelburne and Prof. Knight in the following shops on days mentioned at the noon hour. Reeves Stacker Works, Tuesday and Friday. Reeves Pulley Works, Wednesday and Saturday. Mooney's Tannery on Thursday. Evangelist Shelburne and Prof. Knight enjoy the distinction of conducting the largest shop meetings in America. Mr. Shelburne's helper, Robt. Knight, is one of the best song leaders and soloists in the country. It is but natural to expect that the men in Columbus have a great treat in store for them.

The Hopper
The Republic. April 18, 1907 p. 8
Frank Miller, who was stenographer at Mooney's Tannery, left this morning for South Bend, where he will assume his duties as stenographer for the Studebaker Company, of that city.

At the Churches
The Republic. April 26, 1907 p. 5
[...] The shop meeting was at Mooney's Tannery and the same was well attended, fully 90 per cent. of all the men being in attendance. The meeting today was at Caldwell & Drake's. To-morrow the meeting will be held at the handle factory.

Good Time Given to Ohio Visitors
The Republic. May 14, 1907 p. 1
Seventeen Automobiles Meet Special Train of Cleveland Men. They Liked Columbus. Many of Them Took a Trip Over the City While Others Were Busy With Clients Here — No Meeting Held.

The Cleveland merchants have come and gone and they carried away with them a very good impression of the city of Columbus. The special which carries these business men on their annual trade extension excursion arrived here shortly behind scheduled time, or about 5:20 o'clock Monday afternoon and the reception committee appointed by Mayor Cochrane was on hands to meet the train.

[...] One visitor used handles from the Columbus Handle & Tool Company exclusively in his business and of course he wanted to see that plant. Others were interested in the Mooney tannery and still others wanted to see the Pulley Company and Reeves & Company.

The Hopper
The Republic. May 22, 1907 p. 8
An affidavit has been filed in Justice Stader's court by Bessie Gibson against her husband James Gibson, an employee of Mooney's tannery, Mooney's charging him with assault and battery. The affidavit told the prosecutor that when her husband came home from his work for dinner a few days ago he assaulted her because she did not have biscuits for dinner.

May Miller Burned; Fire Charmed Away
The Republic. June 7, 1907 p. 1
Little Girl Cries Out in Pain — Old Man Looks in the Bible. Played With Matches Three Children Left at Home — Clothing of Girl Caught Fire — Stripped to Skin She Ran to Home of a Neighbor.

May Miller, the seven-year-old daughter of Mr. and Mrs. Ed Miller, was frightfully burned at her home in East Columbus Thursday afternoon about four o'clock. So far as can be learned a physician was not called to see the child, as the neighbors, and also the mother of the child, resorted to home made remedies, and also to having the fire "charmed" away.

The father of the child is foreman in the yards at the Mooney tannery, and he was away at his work when the accident happened. Mrs. Miller had also gone away from home for a short time and had left May, her brother, Willie, aged nine, and a little baby just old enough to walk, at home, is supposed that the children found some matches and began playing with them. At any rate, the clothing worn by the little girl caught fire and she came near being burned to death. Her brother grabbed at the burning clothes and even the little girl showed presence of mind enough to help tear the clothing from her body. The children kept on tearing at the burning clothes until the little girl was stripped naked. She was screaming in pain and the little boy brought a dress skirt of his mother's which he wrapped around the naked body of the girl. The child then ran screaming to the home of the Rev. James Sims, near by. Mr. Sims went to the house, as did also several women who had heard the screams of the child. Mr. Sims wanted to call a physician, but the women are said to have demurred at that, and someone went after the child's mother. Mr. Sims went to the home of a Mr. Buckley, an aged man who lives in East Columbus, and, asked him what was good for burns. Mr. Buckley took his Bible and hunted for a verse which he said was good to take the fire out. He was unable to find the verse for which he was looking, and in the meantime some one had sent for Mrs. Jones, a woman who, it was claimed, had the power to charm away the fire. Mrs. Jones only stopped to put on a clean apron, after which she hurried to the child. The little girl's mother had arrived by that time and had carried the child back home. Mrs. Jones went to the Miller home, where several women had congregated, and proceeded to work her charm. She bent over the child and said some mysterious words which were not revealed to the audience. Mr. Sims went back to hoeing his potatoes.

During all this performance the child had been crying out in pain, but some of the women insist that the child became easier after Mrs. Jones had "charmed the fire away." Later it is reported that linseed oil was applied to the burned places. The child was badly burned about the breast, arms, hands and face. She was thought to be in a serious condition Thursday evening, but this morning she was thought to be doing as well as could be expected.

The Hopper
The Republic. June 20, 1907 p. 8
It was a large bunch of humanity that crowded the Sanitarium lot last night to see the Buckskin Ben Wild West Show, Dog, Pony and Monkey Circus. Of course a great many people went simply for the purpose of looking around and hearing the speilers but a great many patronized the shows and the management had no kick coming on the business done last night. The Buckskin Ben aggregation differs but little from the ordinary carnival. There is the big Wild West show and a number of others. Each show has a speiler in front and even after the crowds begin to thin out people several squares away can hear

the band playing lively tunes while the men with the megaphones bally-hoo in front of their respective shows. A large crowd saw the balloon ascension yesterday afternoon The man in the parachute came down safely in a small field back of the Mooney tannery.

The Hopper
The Republic. July 18, 1907 p. 8
Two colored men, Bedford House and John Ritchie, engaged in a dispute at Mooney's tannery, where they were employed, Wednesday, which resulted in a fight, and the fight resulted in their discharge. After their discharge the men renewed their quarrel and a butcher knife and a piece of lead pipe were flourished in the trouble, but no blood was let at the second quarrel.

Auto Burns While Wrong Number Hits
The Republic. August 14, 1907 p. 1
Trouble With Fire Alarm Causes Department to Go to Tannery. Nineteen Out of Order. First Time New Box Had Ever Been Pulled for a Fire and Registered Wrong — Whistle Goes Up — Falls on Roof.

While Frank Clevenger's Oldsmobile runabout burned to almost a crisp on north Washington street Tuesday afternoon about four o'clock, the fire boys were racing to Mooney's tannery from where they thought a fire alarm had come. Box No. 19 on north Washington street had been pulled but on account of crossed wires or some other trouble the alarm came in from

Box 17, that being the tannery number and the department naturally went there.

Mr. Clevenger was riding along in his machine when he noticed some explosions that did not sound natural. He stopped the machine and started to look at the engine when he found the interior of the auto afire. There were fire gallons of gasoline in the tank and this fed the flames to such an extent that the machine was soon a total wreck. The machine was insured so Mr. Clevenger does not think he will suffer any money loss.

As soon as the automobile was discovered to be afire someone pulled No. 19, that being the first time this box has ever been pulled for a fire. Three weeks ago the box was tested and some trouble was found with it. Fire Chief Doup found after some investigation that wire had been wrapped around the alarm wire, thus grounding it. He cleared the trouble and on the next test No. 19 came in all right. Tuesday afternoon, however, the indicator at the fire department did not register correctly and finally after it had been pulled down once or twice No. 17 registered. The department then hurried to the Mooney tannery only to find that No. 17 had not been pulled and that there was no fire there. Capt. Hendricks then went to Box No. 16 and found that no alarm had been turned in there. It was not until some time later that the department learned of the automobile blaze and that the real alarm had been turned in from No. 19. [...]

Jacob Slooter is Taken Suddenly Ill

The Republic. September 19, 1907 p. 1

And Expires Within Six Hours — Remains Are to be Shipped to Holland, Mich., for Burial.

Jacob Slooter, aged thirty-nine years and unmarried, died suddenly at six o'clock Saturday evening at his room on Fifth street between Washington and Jackson streets and the remains will be shipped this evening to Holland, Mich., the former home of the deceased, for burial.

The deceased was a tanner and was employed at Mooney's tannery, he having come here and accepted a position at the tannery on the third of last July. He was a life long friend of Mr. and Mrs. Ralph Borgman, by whom he was highly esteemed for his many excellent qualities and his gentlemanly bearings on all occasions. Since coming to Columbus he boarded with Mr. and Mrs. Borgman. He was a member of the fraternity of Odd Fellows and had his membership in the Redwood City, Cal., lodge. He was a genial, companionable man and during his short stay in Columbus he made friends of all with whom he came in intimate contact.

He was taken ill at noon last Saturday and while physicians were hastily summoned they were unable to save him and he expired six hours later.

Grand View

The Republic. November 6, 1907 p. 3

It is said that Thomas Moore will remove to Columbus soon, where he has a position in Money's tannery.

Wind is Knocked Out of Leonard Walters

The Republic. November 13, 1907 p. 1

At the Moonery Tannery, and for Time It Was Thought that He Was Killed — Was Pulling Truck.

Leonard Walters, aged nineteen years, who is employed at the Mooney tannery, and lives with his parents, Mr. and Mrs. William Walters, met with an accident at the tannery this morning, and for a time it was thought that he was dead. The young man was walking backwards and pulling a truck which was loaded with hides, when he slipped and fell heavily to the floor. One of the handles of the truck struck him on the stomach and breast and for a half hour he was unconscious.

Dr. John Little Morris was summoned and attended the injured youth. While his injury seemed to be serious at first he shortly recovered from the effects of it and there is now no fear that it will prove fatal. The injured youth is one of the three Walters boys who had the smallpox a few years ago and the disease left its impress on each of the patients.

Augustus Kinsel is Seriously Injured

The Republic. January 8, 1908 p. 1
While Oiling a Splitting Machine at Money's Tannery and Loses Two Fingers in Accident.

Augustus Kinsel, who resides on Eighth street and who is assistant superintendent at Mooney's tannery, met with a distressing accident while working in the line of his duties at the tannery Tuesday afternoon. Mr Kinsel was oiling a splitting machine when the fingers of his left hand were caught by some cogs in the machine and two of his fingers were completely severed from the hand and the ends of the other two fingers were also mashed off by the cogs of the machine.

The injured man went to the office of Dr. Holder, where his hurts were treated and dressed by Dr. Holder.

Young Woman is Stopped by Man

The Republic. January 15, 1908 p. 1
Miss May Tirtle Accosted by a Stranger Close to Heart of the City. He Said "I Want You." Stranger Was a Young Man, Tall and Slim, Attired in a Light Suit, and Wore a Light Hat — Another Woman's Experience.

Miss May Tirtle, who is employed as a stenographer at the Mooney tannery, was followed by a strange young man as she was on her way from the tannery to her home on Sycamore street Tuesday night, and it was only after she screamed and ran into Joseph Trenkenshuh's grocery store that she escaped.

Miss Tirtle had been delayed at the tannery with her work until about 6 o'clock in the evening. She left the office and started east on Fifth street about that time. When near the Dunlap planing mill, on Fifth street, a young man stepped from behind a pile of lumber and started to follow the young woman. He followed Miss Tirtle across Washington and Franklin streets and then, after hurriedly catching up with her he grabbed her by the arm and said, "I want you." Miss Tirtle was badly frightened, but tried to make the man understand that he was mistaken in the person and that he did not want to talk to her. The man insisted that he knew whom he was talking to, and continued to hold Miss Title's arm. She began screaming then, and after a short struggle managed to get away. She ran to the Trenkenshuh grocery, where she telephoned for her sisters to come after her, and after they had come to her aid she continued her way home without being molested further.

The man who accosted Miss Tirtle was not over twenty-two or twenty-three years old, she thinks. He was tall and slim and was attired in a light suit of clothes and a light soft hat. He was a stranger to Miss Tirtle, but she believes she would know him if she were to see him again. The moon was shining bright at the time the affair took place, within a square, almost, of Washington street.

This practice of stopping young women on the streets of Columbus is getting to be a rather common occurrence. Sunday night a well-known young woman in this city was on her way to see a lady friend on south Jackson street, when a man seemed to rise out of the ground and accosted her. She took to her heels at once and as she happened to be near the home of her friend she escaped. A large sized dose of buckshot, administered every few minutes until the desired results are achieved, would be excellent treatment for the young men of Columbus who are making a practice of stopping women on the streets.

The Hopper
The Republic. March 30, 1908 p. 8
William Jones, who is employed at Money's tannery, was jailed Sunday afternoon on a charge of intoxication, but was released on bond a few hours later. He pleaded guilty to the charge in Justice Stader's court this morning and was fined $1 and costs, which he stayed.

The Hopper
The Republic. May 6, 1908 p. 8
Hamilton Marvin, who is employed in the office of the Mooney tannery here, received a telegram this morning telling of the death of his mother at Statesville, N. C. He left at once for that place to attend the funeral.

Additional Hoppers
The Republic. June 13, 1908 p. 4

Bink Schnur has been engaged to repaint the sign on the east side of Mooney's tannery. This sign is 500 feet in length and is said to be one of the longest signs in the state.

[untitled]
The Republic. June 13, 1908 p. 1

While bathing in the old swimming hole in the rear of the Mooney tanners Monday afternoon, Frank Labar stepped on a large thorn, which penetrated his foot to such a depth that it was necessary to use tweezers to draw it out. The wound inflicted by the thorn is a very painful one.

His Memory Failed Him
The Republic. June 13, 1908 p. 5

The police were called to Robert Brown's saloon on south Washington street, Saturday night, and as a result of the call Cleve Brooks was jailed and affidavits were filed against him and David Crouch. The affidavits charge Crouch with assault and battery and Brooks with profanity. Crouch is, said to have assaulted Brooks in Brown's saloon and while acting in the capacity of a peace maker Brown is said to have been knocked down by Crouch, but when asked this morning by the officers who knocked him down, he said that he did not remember who did it.

Shortly after his arrest Brooks put up a cash bond for his appearance in court this morning and was released, but he failed to appear, and his bond was forfeited. Brooks is employed at the Mooney tannery.

Man Handy with Guns Arrested
The Republic. August 24, 1908 p. 1

Man Handy With Guns Arrested. Schroyer's Objections to Garage Get Him Into Trouble. Had Threatened Lives. Prisoner Who is Said to Have Killed Two Men is Thought to Be Mentally Deranged Made Few Few Acquaintances.

Alex Schroyer, a sort of recluse and non-communicative individual, who for the past three years has been "batching" in an upstairs room in the Schwartzkopf block on Jackson street, was arrested and jailed by Marshal Horton and the police Wednesday evening. The prisoner is said to have threatened the lives of persons in the neighborhood of his room, and the one against whom he seems to hold the most malice is Len Benefiel, who has a garage beneath Schroyer's room. He seems determined that Benefiel shall move from his present location and In an effort to accomplish this he is said to have repeatedly threatened Beneflel's life.

[...] Since coming here he has been employed from time to time at the Mooney tannery and at the Reeves Pulley Works.

Two Colored Men with Carnival Co.
The Republic. September 14, 1908 p. 1
Two Colored Men With Carnival Co. Are Charged With Criminal Conduct With a Thirteen-year-old Girl. One of Them Arrested. Joseph Gowdy is Jailed, but Vestal Johnson Makes Good His Escape — Both Men Live at Indianapolis.

Considerable excitement was created among the colored people of Columbus Saturday night, when Thomas Edwards, colored man on north Jackson street, announced that a criminal assault had been committed on his thirteen-year-old daughter Vada by Joseph Gowdy, aged nineteen, and Vestal Johnson, two colored men who were with the Miller Amusement Company, a street carnival company which completed a week's stand here Saturday night.

[...] The little Edwards girl has no mother and when her father, who is employed at Money's tannery, is at his work the child is left alone. Several times last week the two accused colored men called at the Edwards home in the absence of Edwards and on one occasion they were driven from the Edwards home by neighbors, so suspicious had their actions become in connection with the little girl. [...]

The Hopper
The Republic. October 7, 1908 p. 8
Cleve Brooks, who is employed at Mooney's tannery, was taken into Justice Kines's court this morning on a charge of assault and battery on his wife, Lena Brooks, by Marshal Horton. He pleaded guilty to the

charge and was fined one dollar and costs, which was stayed.

Additional Hoppers
The Republic. October 22, 1908 p. 8
A report was in circulation here to-day that Frank Chase, for many years a resident of this city, and an employee of the Mooney tannery, had either been killed or seriously injured by a train at Lewis Creek, in Shelby county. No amount of inquiry here could bring any details of the death or injury of the man to light.

Brough Here for Burial
The Republic. October 24, 1908 p. 5
The body of the late Frank Chase was brought here from Breese, Ill., this morning for burial. It was taken to the morgue of Davidson & Henderson, where services were held at 2 o'clock this afternoon. Burial was in the city cemetery.

Mr. Chase was for many years a resident of this city and worked at the Mooney tannery a long term of years. He was a cousin of the late Salmond P. Chase, who was secretary of the treasury under Lincoln. This week his dead body was found beside the railroad track at Breese, Ill., and it is supposed that he was struck by passing train while standing too near the track. The body was accompanied here by his niece and her husband, Dr. and Mrs. J. C. Eberhart, of Lewis Creek, Shelby county.

Dr. Eberhart went to Illinois and brought the body back to this city.

After Half a Century a Bullet Gets Busy
The Republic. October 28, 1908 p. 1
Howard Marvin is Accidentally Shot Through Hand While Inspecting Primitive Weapon.

With a revolver that had probably been loaded for half a century Howard Marvin, a bookkeeper at Mooney's tannery, and who boards at the Linton home on Third street, was accidentally shot through one of his hands Tuesday evening. The revolver was an old fashioned four-chamber affair and it had lain around the Linton home for many years. In fact its presence had not been known for many years until Tuesday evening, when it was accidentally discovered. Mr. Marvin took possession of the weapon and was in the act of ascertaining if it was still in working order and while in the effort the weapon was accidentally discharged and the bullet plowed through one of his hands.

The wound was dressed by Dr. George T. Mac-Coy, who was not a little surprised to learn that the revolver by which the wound was inflicted was formerly the property of Dick Linton, who was in the same company in the civil war with Dr. MacCoy. Mr. Linton, who is long since deceased, obtained the weapon on the Gulf of Mexico while he was soldiering in the civil war and since that time it has contained the bullet which passed through Mr. Marvin's hand.

County Ticket is a Good One

The Republic. October 31, 1908 p. 1
Republicans Ought to Support Candidates From Top to Bottom. Every Man a Clean One.

[...] Next on the ticket is Roy W. Emig, the candidate for representative. If there is a man on the ticket that deserves to win it is Roy Emig. Born here, reared here, a resident of this county all his life, a young man with clean hands, comes asking for a seat in the lower house of the general assembly and the [illegible] he has made, here, there and everywhere, is abundant assurance of his success next Tuesday. Mr. Emig knows what the working men need. He has worked with his hands, much of his life was spent on a farm. Two years he worked at the local canning factory and a year and a half were spent at Mooney's tannery. He has taught school and knows the educational needs of the county. In every way he deserves to win and he will win if he is given the loyal support of the party which nominated him. [...]

The Hopper

The Republic. December 3, 1908 p. 5
Mooney's tannery postcards at H. M. Holmes[1].

---

[1] Editor's Note: identical item appears in *The Republic* on December 4 and December 5, 1908.

Farmers Coming Here Next Week
The Republic. December 3, 1908 p. 7
Farmers Coming Here Next Week. Their Wives and Children Will Also Attend the Annual Institute. Good Program is Out.

Farmers and their wives, likewise their sons and daughters, are awaiting with a great deal of eagerness for the annual meeting of the Bartholomew County Farmers' Institute and the Woman's Auxiliary, the latter being held in connection with the institute proper. The dates are next Tuesday and Wednesday, December 15 and 16, and the place is the city hall.

[...] For the best collection of wheat the Mooney tannery offers a $5 pair of shoes with Mooney leather soles. [...]

John McComas Dead
The Republic. December 19, 1908 p. 4
John McComas died suddenly at his home on Maple avenue this morning about 9 o'clock. He was sitting in his chair, smoking his pipe, when he collapsed. He was hurriedly placed on a bed, but he did not breathe after that. Heart failure was the cause of his death.

Mr. McComas had been employed at the Mooney tannery for several years and was a valued man there. He had not been feeling well for the past few days and laid off until he should feel better. This morning he felt in his usual health and said he thought he would return to work Monday morning. He died a short time later.

The announcement of the funeral will be made later.

Funeral of John McComas

The Republic. December 21, 1908 p. 8

The funeral of the late John McComas, who died at his home, 626 Maple avenue, suddenly Saturday, will be held from the residence Tuesday afternoon at 2:30 o'clock, conducted by the Rev. Z. T. Sweeney, and burial will be in the City cemetery, under the auspices of Columbus Lodge No. 58, I. O. O. F.

Mr. McComas was an employee of the Mooney tannery for more than thirty years and the men there have made up a purse of $40 which they will expend for a floral tribute to send to the funeral.

The Hopper

The Republic. December 29, 1908 p. 8

Louis Houk, who was employed at the Mooney tannery, has resigned his position and has moved with his family to the Howard J. Tooley farm in the west part of the county.

Free Water Grant Will Soon Expire

The Republic. February 6, 1909 p. 4

There Will Be No Free Water in Columbus After Next Year Unless Franchise is Extended.

The water will be shut off for two or three hours in the neighborhood of Reeves & Co.'s factory tomorrow morning while a large Lambert water meter is being put in at the Reeves factory, and this recalls the fact that at the Reeves & Co. factory and the Reeves Pulley Works are the only places in the city at which water meters are in use in the city of Columbus. All other water consumers are given a flat rate with the exception of all other factories and some other industries which have been granted free water by the city. The two Reeves factories are the only ones in the city that are paying the city for the water used by them.

However, in 1910 there will be no free water in Columbus unless the city chooses to renew the present free water franchises, for in that year the free water franchises will expire. Among the factories and other industries now receiving free water from the city are Mooney's tannery, the Handle and Tool Company, the Columbus ice plant, Glanton's and the Orinoco furniture factories, the Caldwell & Drake Iron Works, the Caldwell Manufacturing Company, Hege & Co. Dunlap & Co. some of the mills and elevators of the city and the hoop factory, etc.

Fifteen-Year-Old Husband is In Jail
The Republic. February 17, 1909 p. 1
For Beating His 17-Year-Old Wife, Who Appeared in Court with Evidence of Blow on Either Cheek.

The marriage of two children, Vernon Stidd, aged fifteen, and Hazel Allen, aged seventeen years, which was solemnized on December 22 last, has thus early proved a failure and the youthful husband is in jail for beating his youthful wife.

Stidd was arrested Tuesday night by Officer Garrison and taken into Justice Kinney's court, where he gave bond for his appearance in court at 9 o'clock this morning. His trial was had this morning and the defendant was convicted. He was fined $1 and costs and in default of the amount he was sent to jail. The young wife appeared against her husband and the condition of her face was the best testimony introduced in her favor, for it was evident that a blow had been struck on each cheek. She said her husband struck her twice. The husband admitted that he struck her, but said they were scuffling in fun when each got mad.

Justice Kinney and Officer Garrison attempted a good Samaritan stunt by advising the couple to drop the matter and kiss and make up, but each stood pat on their hostile attitudes with the result that the husband went to jail. Stidd is employed at the Mooney tannery and the couple live at Sixth and Wilson streets.

Additional Hoppers
The Republic. February 22, 1909 p. 4
One of the upper floors, sixteen feet square, in Mooney's tannery collapsed Sunday and fell to the floor below, carrying with it a large quantity of leather which was stored in the room. The weight of the leather caused the floor to collapse. Fortunately there was no one on the lower floor and no one was hurt.

Grant Petition of the Firemen
The Republic. March 30, 1909 p. 1
Farmers Coming Here Next Week. Their Wives and Children Will Also Attend the Annual Institute. Good Program is Out.

[...] On first alarms No. 1 will respond to boxes 12, 13, 14, 15, 16, 17, 19, 21, 23, 84, 85, 26, 31, 34, 42, 43, 45 and 46. Company No. 2 will respond on first alarms to the following boxes: Nos. 17, 35, 36, 37, 58, 53, 54, 56 and 57. Both companies will respond to alarms from No. 4 at Reeves & Co. No. 5 at Reeves Pulley Company and No. 17 at the Mooney tannery. The ordinance as originally prepared only provided for both companies answering the alarms from No. 4 and No. 5, but the measure was changed last night so that both departments would go to No. 17 on first alarms. Both companies will respond to all second alarms anywhere in the city.

Additional Hoppers
The Republic. May 1, 1909 p. 4
George P. Herndon, one of the officials of the Mooney tannery, this afternoon purchased 160 acres of land owned by Mrs. Lizzie Boyd in Jackson township for $4,400, an average of $27.50 per acre. This is the cheapest farm land sold in this county in a long time. The land was sold at auction in the court house corridor and strenuous efforts were made by Auctioneer Irvin A. Cox to raise the price. However, $27.50 was

as high a price per acre as could be secured and the land was knocked down to Mr. Herndon for that figure.

The Hoppers
The Republic. May 17, 1909 p. 8
Elmer Moore left last night to cover northern Indiana and Michigan territory for the Mooney tannery. Mr. Moore will travel for the local tannery in the future.

Special Policeman Arrests a Stranger
The Republic. May 25, 1909 p. 8
Who Tells Straight Story of Himself and is Relieved After Being Questioned at Mayor's Office.

William Western, one of the several special policemen who have been deputized since the big burglar scare struck Columbus, arrested a stranger north of the city Monday and marched him to the mayor's office, where be was closely questioned and released. The special officer said his attention was attracted to the stranger by his suspicious actions while in the city, and he followed him a considerable distance north of the city, where he arrested him and brought him back. He said that when the man discovered that he was being followed he tried several times to hide and otherwise acted as if he did not wish to be seen or taken.

At the mayor's office the stranger, who was an Austrian, told in badly broken English a straight story of himself, which effected his release. He said he had formerly worked at Money's tannery and had returned here in the hope of again getting work, but having failed he had started to walk to Indianapolis when he was arrested.

Personals
The Republic. June 16, 1909 p. 8
Elmer Moore left last evening for a trip through Illinois in the interest of the Mooney tannery.

The Hopper
The Republic. September 7, 1909 p. 8
Fred Wetzel, who has been employed at Mooney's tannery for about fifteen years, has been given a position as manager of the tannery company's plant at Elizabethtown, Tenn., and he will shortly move with his family to that place.

The Hopper
The Republic. September 27, 1909 p. 8
The case of James C. Hill against the Mooney tannery for $5,000 damages, in which a change of venue was granted on the affidavit of Hill, has been sent to Johnson county for trial.

Charles S. Barnaby Says He Will Enforce the Law
The Republic. October 4, 1909 p. 1, 5
Charles S. Barnaby Says He Will Enforce the Law. Popular Man at Head of Ticket. Republicans Name Unusually Strong Candidates in Harmonious Meet. Cobb Named for Clerk

The ticket: For Mayor — Charles S. Barnaby; For Clerk — Edwin A. Cobb; For Treasurer — Elmer E.

Godfrey; For Councilmen-at-Large — Henry Stahlbuth and George P. Herndon.

[...] The two nominations for councilmen-at-large are admirable in every way. Mr. Herndon as superintendent of the Mooney tannery has held a responsible position where only a man of sound judgment could remain. He knows the needs of the city and he is able to give the city a clean and progressive administration. Mr. Stahlhuth is one of the best known Germans in the city. He is employed at the plant of the Reeves Pulley Company, where he is one of the company's most valued and efficient workmen, and he has made such a study of city affairs that he knows what the city needs. So it is from top to bottom and from bottom back to top again the Republicans have a ticket of which they may well feel proud. There is not a weak place in it and from now on it will be merely a question of how big a majority the republicans care to pile up when November 2 comes.

The Hopper
The Republic. October 11, 1909 p. 4
Guy Kelley, who was sentenced to the Indiana state prison at Michigan City in the Bartholomew Circuit Court for larceny, has been paroled and arrived home Sunday. He is now employed at the Mooney tannery.

Henry Brunting Died Suddenly

The Republic. October 11, 1909 p. 5

Veteran Expressman Victim of Heart Failure This Afternoon. Lived Here Long Time. Had Been in Poor Health for Some Time and Was Making Arrangements to Retire From Express Business — Had Many, Friends.

Henry Bruning, the veteran expressman, died suddenly this afternoon. It was reported that he had hitched up for the afternoon and had started to drive down town from his home on Union street when he suffered an attack of heart failure and fell dead. Hendersons & Hathaway, undertakers, were notified, and it was said late this afternoon that the coroner would be called.

Mr. Bruning was born in Germany but came to this country many years ago. For a long time he worked at the Mooney tannery but for the past twenty or more years he had been driving an express wagon. Only recently he decided to sell the horses and wagon and retire from business. He said he was not feeling well here of late and had made up his mind to take a rest. He was out with his wagon this morning, and almost every day recently but this afternoon the trouble with his heart grew worse and the end came quickly.

Mr. Bruning was a brother of John Bruning, of this city, and leaves a son and daughter. His wife died a few years ago.

Almost every man, woman and child knew Henry Bruning. He had been a fixture in the life of this city for so long and his friends were so many that the news of his depth will come as a genuine shock. For years he made his headquarters down town at the Leinberger tailoring establishment, where he liked to spend his idle moments discussing various problems of the day. He was firm In his beliefs and ever ready to stand behind what he said. He was a man that will be missed by many people here and one who was good at heart, honest, kindly and good natured.

The Hopper
The Republic. November 9, 1909 p. 8
Walter Temple, who has been employed at Mooney's tannery, has secured a position as brakeman on the Indianapolis Southern railroad and will leave tomorrow morning for Indianapolis to enter on his new duties.

Pleasure Seeker Dies in Patrol
The Republic. November 30, 1909 p. 1
Ignatz Huber Taken Suddeniy Ill While on Cincinnati Excursion. No Relatives Found. Donation is Made Up at Mooney's Tannery and Body Will Be Brought to Columbus for Proper Burial.

Ignatz Huber, aged about forty-five years, who was employed at the Mooney tannery, died suddenly at Cincinnati, Ohio, Sunday evening. He had gone to that city on an excursion and was accompanied by David Beabout, also of this city. He was taken suddenly ill shortly before the excursion train was due to leave on the return trip for Columbus and was found lying unconscious on the streets of Cincinnati. He died in the patrol while on the way to a hospital and he was taken to a morgue instead of a hospital.

The next morning Mr. Beabout read of his death in a Cincinnati paper and going to the morgue he identified the body as that of Huber. When he died there was found on his person 72 cents in change, a gold watch and a return ticket from Cincinnati to this city. Mr. Beabout was instructed to come to this city, get the sheriff and coroner and search the dead man's room in an effort to locate some of his relatives. He arrived Monday evening and getting Sheriff Cox and Deputy Coroner Flanigan the room on south Washington street formerly occupied by Huber was entered and thoroughly searched, but nothing was found that would lead to the location of any of the dead man's relatives. A business letter written to him from St. Louis, Mo., to Springfield, Ohio, in 1906 and naturalization papers issued at St. Louis, Mo, in 1896 were all the papers of any importance that were found in the room.

The dead man had $50 in the People's Bank and this morning a sufficient amount additional was made up at the Mooney tannery to defray the expenses of bringing the body to this city and giving it proper burial. Huber had been in Columbus for two years and was well liked at the Mooney tannery, where he has worked since coming here.

Card of Thanks
The Republic. December 3, 1909 p. 4
We are sincerely thankful to Dr. A. K. Mattingly and J. D. Emmons & Co. for their kindly an efficient services at the funeral of our fellow workman, Ignatz Huber.

Employees of Money's Tannery.

The Hopper
The Republic. December 8, 1909 p. 8
Frederick Leibrock, who is employed at the Mooney tannery, left to-day for his home near Pirmasons, in the Rheinish Palestine. His family has been living there since he has been in America. He is now going to close up his affairs in Germany and bring his family to Columbus, where they will live.

Lyle Wert Victim of Heart Disease
The Republic. January 22, 1910 p. 1
Lyle Wert Victim of Heart Disease. Promising and Well Known Young Resident of This City Died After Short Illness This Morning.

After an illness of short duration that first seemed slight and then rapidly developed alarming features, Lyle Wert died at the home of his parents, Mr. and Mrs. Charles Wertz, at Fifteenth and Washington Streets, this morning at 7:30 o'clock. Acute heart trouble was the cause of his death.

The late Mr. Wert was born in Columbus twenty-six years ago, his twenty-sixth birthday having been on the ninth day of this month. He spent practically all of his young life in Columbus. After having attended the local schools he took employment here and later held a responsible position at the Mooney tannery, where he was considered one of the most valued workmen of the entire force.

Early in life he united with the Presbyterian church and continued a member of that faith. He was also a member of the local lodge of Elks. Because of the youth of Mr. Wert, and because of the fact that his home life was so happy and his future so bright, his death is unusually sad. His friends among the people of this city, both young and old, could hardly be counted and expressions of sorrow over his death and of sympathy for the bereaved family were heard on every hand today.

Mr. Wert possessed a tenor voice of great range and power and his singing had frequently been heard here in times past not only in church choirs but in home talent productions and home talent concerts.

The funeral will be held from the residence Monday afternoon at 2 o'clock, conducted by Dr. Alfred H. Pitkin, with the Rev. James Comfort rector of St. Paul's church, assisting burial will, be in the Garland Brook cemetery.

Eighteen Inches and Five Below
The Republic. February 18, 1910 p. 1
Snow Foot and Half Deep and Weather Severe is the Local Story. Trains Have Bad Luck. Big Four Ran Into Snow Drift Near Hope and Was Out All Night Traction Cars Delayed — Damage to Roof at Tannery.

[...] The heavy load of snow on the roof of the Mooney tannery caused a slight cave-in, but the damage done was small. [...]

The Hopper
The Republic. February 18, 1910 p. 8
Ed Miller, who for several years was employed at the Mooney tannery has returned to Columbus with his family from Terre Haute and has again taken employment at the tannery.

The Hopper
The Republic. February 18, 1910 p. 6
Charles Meyers, an employee of the Mooney tannery, was painfully injured yesterday. He was working at one of the machines in the plant when one hand was caught and the ends of the fingers cut off.

Many Taxpayers Were Missedy by Accessors
The Republic. July 7, 1910 p. 8
In Columbus Last Year and One Hundred and Fifty of Them Lived in Maple Grove and Orinoco.

That the tax assessment of the city of Columbus was somewhat incomplete last year is shown by the fact that already one hundred and fifty tax payers in Orinoco and Maple Grove that were missed last year have been placed of the assessment list this year. Township Assessor Ed Hall said this morning that the assessment of the township would be increased $200,000 this year over last year's assessment. This, however, will be due more to the advance that has been made in the assessment rates than to the number of taxpayers who were missed last year and are being found this year.

The Birk boarding house on west Fourth street has not yet been assessed, and when the assessor calls there he will flush by far the biggest covey of taxpayers to be found in any one other house in the city, for there are eighty-five persons to be assessed at that house. Speaking of the Birk boarding house recalls a rather unusual tax incident that occurred at the court house Thursday.

Mrs. John Birk called at the county treasurer's office to pay her taxes, when she told that her husband owed $4.40 taxes. Mrs. Birk called the attention of Township Assessor Hall to the claim and on investigation it was learned that the claim was against John Birk, who is employed at Mooney's tannery, and whose taxes Mrs. Birk has been paying for the past few years, under the belief that she was paving her husband's taxes, who has not been assessed in recent years.

Lona Sweetland Wins the Piano
The Republic. May 2, 1910 p. 8
Lona Sweetland Wins the Piano. Popular Stenographer at Mooney Tannery Lead Gysie Piano Contest. Race a Great Success. Hundreds of Thousands of Votes Cast in Contest That Proved Successful From Start — Miss Sweetland Had Big Lead. The cheers that fairly shook the clothing store of Joseph L. Gysie, about 12 o'clock Saturday night, demonstrated the

result of the piano contest was a popular one. Miss Lona Sweetland won the piano and was without a doubt the happiest girl in Columbus Saturday night. The instrument was moved to her boarding place this morning.

Miss Sweetland is a stenographer at the Mooney tannery and that she is popular was demonstrated by the way she ran in the contest.

Miss Sweetland won the contest with a total of 183,940 votes. Her nearest competitor was the local tribe of Red Men, the total vote of that lodge being 103,220, giving Miss Sweetland a lead of 80,720 votes. The Knights of Pythias lodge finished third and the Odd Fellows lodge fourth. There were seventy-eight contestants and hundreds of thousands of votes were cast. Although the votes came as thick as snow flakes, many were still out when the contest closed, ballot holders having misplaced their votes or else they forgot to vote them.

Mr. Gysie began the piano contest January 8, 1910, and it has been a success from start to finish. He offered to give away a Gilbert upright piano to the person receiving the highest number of votes in the contest and every person who made a purchase at the store got a certain number of ballots to cast. The number of ballots was regulated by the amount of money spent for merchandise. As an advertising feature the contest proved its success early, because the lure of the piano brought new customers to the store and secured purchases from old customers who were either anxious to win the piano for themselves or else were boosting for some friend.

The last vote was cast at 10 o'clock Saturday night, the time announced for the close of the contest, and the judges then began the count. The Judges were Charles Setser, George Stanley, F. M. Blair, and Miss Blanche Smith, and it was almost Sunday when they counted out the winner and made the announcement. A big crowd had packed the store since the time for the contest to close and the people greeted the announcement of Miss Sweetland as the winner with lusty cheers. The contest has been conducted in a fair and impartial manner and there are no sore spots as a result of the wind-up.

Urging Columbus to Show Proper Spirit

The Republic. July 7, 1910 p. 6

Booster for Ohio Valley Exposition Valley Talks to Council and Business Men of This City.

W. P. Whitlock, formerly financial editor of the *Cincinnati Commercial Tribune*, but now a special representative of the Ohio Valley Industrial Exposition, was here last evening evening arousing local interest in the meeting.

The exposition will be held in Cincinnati August 29 to September 24, and the chief aim of those in charge is to bring the rapidly growing South into closer touch with the Ohio valley. Indiana is an important part of the valley, so Mr. Whitlock has been visiting various Indiana cities and towns and telling the people what they will miss if they cross Cincinnati's exposition off their visiting list.

The exposition will have President Taft as a visitor during the first week; Thomas A. Edison during the second week and former President Roosevelt near the close. An added attraction is the Roosevelt trophies of his African hunt. Such trophies as have been mounted will be loaned by the Smithsonian Institute.

A new feature of this exposition will be a propaganda bureau where any city interested in boosting itself will be given free space for literature and advertising matter.

While here Mr. Whitlock addressed the city council and asked for no special action aside from getting things stirred up here so that Columbus might be represented. He talked to President Louis J. Scheidt, of the Comercial Club, and to others, and left a most cordial invitation for Columbus to go down to Cincinnati and feel at home.

Mr. Whitlock collected considerable industrial data during his short visit in Columbus and as a result of his visit he will make efforts to interest such concerns as Reeves & Company, Reeves Pulley Company, The Columbus Handle & Tool Company, the Mooney Tannery, the Orinoco Furniture Company, and others, in making exhibits at the exposition.

Joseph Bennett is Burned by Liquors
The Republic. July 21, 1910 p. 6
Fell Into Leach Tub at Mooney Tannery and Lost All Skin on Both Feet When Pulled Out.

Joseph Bennett, who lives on east Tenth street, fell into a leach tub at the Mooney tannery yesterday afternoon and had both feet badly blistered.

Bennett is a carpenter and was doing some overhead work when he slipped and started to fall into the tub. He grasped some timbers above him and hung suspended with his feet in the steaming liquid until he was rescued. Steam is turned into the leach tubs and the liquid is scalding hot. When Bennett's shoes and socks were removed most of the par-boiled skin came off his feet.

Jacob Beyl is Dead at Home in Columbus
The Republic. October 12, 1910 p. 6
Was Native of France But Had Been in America Since Young — Was Formerly Grocer Here.

Jacob Beyl, who had been a resident of this city for the past thirty years, died at 4:40 o'clock Tuesday afternoon at the family residence, 542 Jackson street. Death was due to a complication of diseases.

Four years ago last August Mr. Beyl was attacked by a paralytic stroke which affected his mind. Since that time he had gradually grown worse until death came.

Mr. Beyl was born in France in 1846. He came to this country with his parents in 1852 and settled in New Orleans, where he resided until he was a young man. While there he ran a steamboat on the Mississippi river. He then came to Indiana and lived on a farm near Memphis for several years. Afterward he gave up farming and went to work on the Pennsylvania railroad. He was night watchman at the Mooney tannery for several years. It was then he started in the grocery business on Third street. He was also constable for two terms. Mr. Beyl was a civil war veteran.

He was married to Margaret Hern in 1872. He leaves a widow and three sons, William, of this city, and Edward and Grover, of Indianapolis, and two daughters, Mrs. Charles Blake and Mrs. Everett Mobley, of Indianapolis, who have been at their father's bedside for a week.

The funeral will be held at the residence on Jackson street Thursday afternoon at 2 o'clock. Services conducted by Rev. I. H. Book, of the Christian church. The remains will be laid to rest in the Garland Drook cemetery.

The Hopper
The Republic. October 12, 1910 p. 8
A. Vanden Ende, formerly connected with the Mooney tannery here, was in Columbus calling on the trade today. He. now represents J. T. Kirkpatrick & Company, dealers in hides and leather, of Philadelphia.

Rufus Snyder Dead

The Republic. October 21, 1910 p. 5

Rufus Snyder, an old resident here, died at his home, 813 Jackson street, Thursday evening at 6 o'clock. He was 70 years old. His wife died about two years ago.

Mr. Snyder was a hard working man and had been a faithful employee of the Mooney tannery for thirty-one years. He is survived by three children, two sons, George and Fred, and a daughter, Mrs. Addie Piper.

The funeral will be held Sunday afternoon at 2 o'clock, conducted by Dr. Alfred H. Pitkin and burial will be in the Garland Brook cemetery.

The Personals

The Republic. October 22, 1910 p. 8

Levi Hege has gone to Elizabethton, Tenn., in the interest of the Mooney tannery.

Additional Personals

The Republic. November 8, 1910 p. 8

Tooley, of Brown street, a fireman at the Mooney tannery, accidentally burned one of his fingers on a poker Sunday night. Blood poisoning has set in and his hand is in a serious condition.

Sherman Wooten Gets Peevish When Taken

The Republic. December 6, 1910 p. 8

Into Court on Charge of Intoxication and Berates Everybody Connected With His Arrest.

Sherman Wooten, of Thirteenth street, who is employed at the Mooneys tannery, was jailed on a charge of intoxication Monday night and when he was arraigned in Mayor Barnaby's court this morning he appeared to be very much put out because of his arrest, and in fact he was much peeved and berated everybody connected with his arrest, saying that it was an imposition. He said he was not intoxicated, yet he admitted that he might have been a little full, but insisted that he was on his way home and was pestering no one.

When told that he must stay, lay, or pay his fine the prisoner said he would ask no one to stay his fine, but when and officer started to jail with him he changed his mind and procured a stay.

Falling Pen Knife Severs and Artery

The Republic. December 10, 1910 p. 4

William A. Mooney Suffered From Loss of Blood From an Injury Inflicted in Unusual Manner.

William A. Mooney was injured in an unusual manner this morning at his office at the Mooney tannery. He accidentally severed an artery in one knee with a penknife and Dr. A. J. Banker had to be called to stop the flow of blood.

Mr. Mooney was opening letters with his knife when it slipped from his hand and started to drop to the floor. He instinctively brought his knees together to catch the knife and in this manner one knee struck the falling knife and jabbed the blade into the other knee. An artery was severed and there was a considerable loss of blood before the surgeon arrived.

mogtus sanlux

publisher

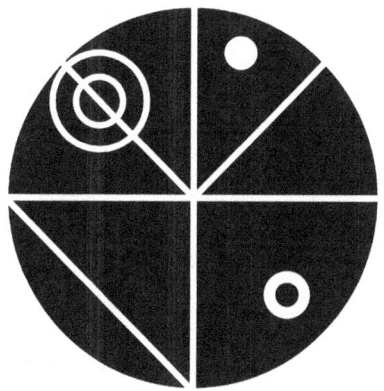

"A procession of the damned. By the damned, I mean the excluded. We shall have a procession of data that Science has excluded. Battalions of the accursed, captained by pallid data that I have exhumed, will march. You'll read them — or they'll march. Some of them livid and some of them fiery and some of them rotten."

Charles Fort
The Book of the Damned

Public catalog: mogtus-sanlux.one
Private catalog: ~mogtus-sanlux

Index

Abbott, Edgar, 107
Adams, Will, 30
Aickle, Julia, 93
Aikens, W. W., 36
Allen, Hazel Allen, 137, 138
Apel, (Mrs.) Charles, 80
Arnold, J. W., 61, 94

Banker, A. J., 109, 115, 156
Barnaby, Charles S., 141, 156
Bassett, E. H., 89
Beabout, David, 144, 145
Beam, Samuel, 43
Bearhope, George, 85
Bearhope, Richard, 85, 113
Beasecker, S. B., 79
Beatty, Frank, 33
Beck, W. J., 88
Benefiel, Len, 130
Benham, J. W., 95
Bennett, Joseph, 153
Beveridge, A. J., 83
Bevis, Harry, 102
Beyl, Edward, 154
Beyl, Grover, 154
Beyl, Jacob, 153
Beyl, William, 154
Birk, (Mrs.) John, 149
Birk, John, 149
Blair, F. M., 151
Bolinger, Amos, 85
Bonham, John, 8, 9
Book, (Mrs.), 103
Book, I. H., 154
Book, William H., 100, 103
Borgman, (Mrs.) Ralph, 124

Borgman, Ralph, 124
Bosswell, Jacob, 108
Box, (Undertaker), 5, 6
Boyd, B. M., 89
Boyd, Lizzie, 139
Boyd, S. B., 35
Brandt, Sarah, 92
Brinkley, William, 65
Brockman, George, 50
Brooks, Cleve, 129, 131
Brooks, Lena, 131
Brown, Robert, 129
Bruning, Henry, 143, 144
Bruning, John, 143
Brunswick, Dave, 67
Buckley, (Mr.), 120
"Buckskin Ben", 121
Burk, George, 93, 94
Burtch, (Rev. Mr.), 115

Caldwell, George W., 23, 33, 35, 54, 58
Campbell, H. M., 89
Campbell, Ruby, 102
Carnaban, (Comm. / Gen'l), 10, 11
Carr, (Councilman), 21, 56
Carr, Herman, 38, 55, 59
Carry, Will, 49
Carter, George W., 85
Chase, Frank, 132
Chase, Salmond P., 132
Clark, Newton, 23, 81
Clevenger, Frank, 122, 123
Coats, Frank, 33–35
Cobb, Edwin A., 47, 141
Cochrane, (Mayor), 118

Columbus, Christopher, 71
Comfort, James, 147
Cooper, Geo. W., 19
Cooper, John, 85
Cox, Irvin A., 139, 145
Creath, Amos S., 17
Crouch, David, 129
Crow, Dan, 34
Crump, F. T., 17, 27–29
Curry, Will, 52
Cusson, Napoleon, 18

Dalgetta-Kerr, George, 27, 71
Davis, Jesse, 85
Davis, John, 47
Donaker, (City Attorney), 32
Doup, (Fire Chief), 123
Dowell, W. H., 33
Drake, Lester, 34
Dryden, Dr. / Councilman, 49, 55, 56, 100
Dungan, Z. T., 57

Earl, E. E., 98, 99
Eberhart, (Mrs.) J. C., 132
Eberhart, J. C., 132
Edison, Thomas A., 152
Edwards, Thomas, 131
Edwards, Vada, 131
Emig, Roy W., 134
Emmons, (Councilman), 55, 56
Ende, A. Vanden, 154

Fellows, John T., 85
Ferguson, (Policeman), 42
Fisher, George, 54
Flanigan, (Deputy Coroner), 145
Formehlen, (Water-Works Trustee), 17
Frank, A. J., 58

Gable, Joe, 29, 30
Gable, Leoti, 44
Ganes, John, 10
Garrett, Charles, 93, 94
Garrison, (Officer), 138
Gibson, Bessie, 119
Gibson, James, 119
Gilday, John, 37, 38
Gilmore, Albert, 85

Glanton, James, 77
Glanton, Jas. A., 65
Godfrey, (County Clerk), 116
Godfrey, Elmer E., 116, 142
Gordon, C. A., 36
Gowdy, Joseph, 131
Gray, Loa, 52
Greenfield, Daniel, 85
Greenfield, Jr., Dan, 52
Grier, V. L., 34
Griffis, Joseph H., 50
Griffith, H., 41
Grove, Clarence, 51, 60
Gysie, Joseph L., 149, 150

Hack, John A., 52
Haggard, W. H. N., 89
Haigh, S. E., 34, 36
Haislup, John, 44
Hall, Ed, 148, 149
Hall, Stephen, 85
Harper, (Prof.), 34
Harris, Frank, 85
Harvey, F. M., 79
Haycock, Elmer, 103
Heckard, (Dr.), 33
Hege, (Civil Engineer), 32
Hege, Levi, 31, 155
Hendricks, (Captain), 123
Henke, George, 35
Henry, Charles, 112
Henry, James, 21
Henry, Robert M., 85
Hern, Margaret, 154
Herndon, Alva, 85
Herndon, George P., 85, 107, 139, 142
Hill, Frank, 85
Hill, James C., 141
Hingston, John, 96
Hingston, Joseph, 85
Hodler, George, 112
Hofer, John, 95
Holder, (Dr.), 126
Horton, (Marshal), 94, 130, 131
Horton, Ed, 85
Houk, Louis, 136
House, Bedford, 122
Huber, Ignatz, 144–146

INDEX

Huffman, Frank, 41
Hunter, Ellis, 57

Irwin, (Councilman), 24
Irwin, Joseph I., 69
Irwin, Will G., 81

Jacobs, Sarah, 80
Johnson, (Mr.), 115
Johnson, Ben, 115–117
Johnson, Vestal, 131
Jonee, Charlie, 33
Jones, (Mrs.), 120, 121
Jones, B. B., 34
Jones, Roy, 93
Jones, William, 128
Jord, (Judge), 37

Kelble, (Water-Works Committee), 54, 55
Kelley, Guy, 85, 142
Kennard, Frank, 85
Keye, Louise, 102
Keyes, Will, 47
Kines, (Justice), 131
Kinney, (Justice), 138
Kinsel, Gus / Augustus, 46, 126
Kinsel, Walter, 37, 44–46
Kinson, Gus / Augustus, 44
Knight, Robt., 117
Kollmeyer, C. J., 33, 34
Kyte, W. H., 85

Labar, Frank, 129
Lambert, Peter, 86
Lamoreux, F. O., 82
Lash, J. J., 85
Lawhead, Ed, 45, 46
Lawhead, John, 37, 38
Lawless, Samuel, 37, 38
Lefler, Charles, 91, 92
Lefter, Charles, 91
Leibrock, Frederick, 146
Leper, Charles, 61
Lincoln, Abraham, 132
Linton, Dick, 133
Lister, John, 99
Lopp, (Dr.), 34
Lucas, (Mr.), 102
Lucas, George H., 101

Lucas, W. J., 24
Lune, John, 85

MacCaffey, (Baseball), 91
MacCoy, George T., 49, 133
MacKain, J., 51
Mantel, Brown, 102
Manuel, Edna, 114
Marsh, J. N., 34
Marvin, Hamilton, 128
Marvin, Howard, 133
Mattingly, Mattingly, A. K., 146
McBride, (Councilman), 56
McCloskey, A. K., 86
McComas, John, 135, 136
McCormack, P. H., 24, 33–35, 49, 54, 70
McCracken, O. M., 34
McCullough, (Councilman), 32
McKay, Isaac, 82
McKay, Sherman, 82
McMillan, Bert, 85
McNeal, Frank, 33, 35
Meginis, D. H., 5, 6
Mercer, C. S., 71
Meyers, Charles, 148
Miller, (Mrs.), 101
Miller, (Mrs.) Ed, 119, 120
Miller, Charley, 7
Miller, Ed, 119, 148
Miller, Edward, 101
Miller, Frank, 118
Miller, Hugh Th., 106
Miller, James, 85
Miller, Joseph, 85
Miller, Matilda, 93
Miller, May, 119, 120
Miller, W. F., 52
Miller, Willie, 120
Mitchell, (Mrs.), 99
Mitchell, Alpha, 99
Mitchell, Carl, 99
Mitchell, John, 82
Mitchell, William, 27, 83
Mobley, (Mrs.) Everett, 154
Mooney, (Alderman), 1–6
Mooney, Councilman, 21
Mooney, Edward, 33
Mooney, J. E., 7, 10

Mooney, J. H., 13, 14
Mooney, Thomas, 55
Mooney, W. W., 20
Mooney, William A., 17, 36, 51, 54, 96, 156, 157
Moore, Elmer, 48, 60, 140, 141
Moore, Thomas, 125
Morgan John W., 80
Morris, John Little, 109, 125
Mosbaugh, Frank, 51
Mrs, (Mrs.) Charles, 154
Mudd, Anna May, 115–117
Myrers, W. R., 19

Nelson, (Mrs.), 97
Nelson, Albert J., 88
Nelson, Rade M., 88
Noblitt, John, 86

Olay, E., 89
Olmstead, James, 85
Orban, John, 92
Overstreet, Bert, 20

Parker, (Councilman / Mayor), 32
Paschell, Homer, 116, 117
Piper, Addie, 155
Pitkin, Alfred H., 147, 155
Pittman, Sylvia, 112
Poe, Fred, 20
Prather, Littie, 49
Prather, T. B., 49
Pruitt, William, 86
Puris, Bluford, 32

Reeves, (Chief of Fire Department), 17
Reeves, (Councilman), 48, 54–56
Reeves, Gurney L., 51, 63
Reeves, M. O., 89
Reeves, M. T., 89
Reeves, Marshal T., 36
Reeves, Robert, 51
Remy, E. A., 76
Rethwisch, Fred, 41
Rice, (Col.), 8
Rice, (Dr.), 26, 61
Richards, (Rev.), 103
Richards, Charles Gorman, 103
Riley, Lawrence, 8

Ritchie, John, 122
Robinson, Thomas F., 50, 108
Roosevelt, Theodore, 46, 152
Ross, (Mrs.) Charles A., 88
Ross, Jennie, 85
Rost, (Councilman), 32
Roth, J. G., 88
Rudolph, Jeremiah, 48
Rudolph, Wesley, 48

Saladin, Ed, 25, 26
Saladin, Jacob, 25
Sallivan, Alexander, 85
Sanders, Newton, 105
Sattle, F. L., 89
Scheidt, Louis J., 152
Schimner, Moore Tilton, 19
Schinnerer, Christian, 93
Schinnerer, Eva, 92
Schinnerer, John, 92, 93
Schinnerer, Sarah, 92
Schnur, Bink, 129
Schoonover, Jr., Henry, 91, 109
Schowe, Harry, 89
Schroyer, Alex, 130
Schwartzkopf, (Mr.), 25
Scott, Jr., John, 47
Sertz, John, 85
Setser, Charles, 151
Sharp, Jr., J. K., 89
Shelburne, (Evangelist), 117
Shroyer, John, 95
Shultz, Anderson, 59
Sims, James, 120
Slooter, Jacob, 124
Smith, Addie, 102
Smith, Blanche, 113, 151
Smith, Frank, 61
Smith, Joseph, 85
Smith, William, 85
Smiths, George, 85
Snively, Bert, 86
Snively, Smith W., 85
Snyder, Fred, 155
Snyder, George, 155
Snyder, Rufus, 155
Sparrell, C. F., 34
Spencer, (Mayor), 17
Stader, (Justice), 47, 98, 119, 128

Stahlbuth, Henry, 142
Stahlhuth, Ernst, 56
Stanley, George, 151
Starkey, (Baseball), 91
Stevens, John, 85
Stidd, Vernon, 137, 138
Stillablower, Vol, 14–16
Stillinger, Everett, 17
Strauss, A., 33
Swanke, Henrietta, 93
Sweany, Clarence O., 84, 86–88
Sweeney, Z. T., 136
Sweetland, Lona, 149–151

Taft, William Howard, 152
Temple, Walter, 144
Thompson, John, 52
Timbrook, (Mrs.) James, 113, 114
Timbrook, James, 114
Tipton, (General), 58
Tirtle, May, 126, 127
Tompkins, H., 34
Tooley, Howard J., 136, 155
Tormehlen, (Councilman), 55
Trenkenshuh, Joseph, 127
Trotter, (Water-Works Trustee), 17
Troutman, John, 85
Truax, (Mrs.) Ed, 114
Turner, W. E., 37, 38

Van Wye, Carl, 85
Vaughn, William, 86

Wagner, (Mrs.) John, 101
Wagner, R. E., 86

Walford, Augustus E., 85
Wall, (Miss), 71
Walters, (Mrs.) William, 125
Walters, Leonard, 125
Walters, Milton, 111
Walters, William, 125
Warner, John, 110
Way, C. S., 115
Wayt, Addison, 98
Wayt, George, 98
Weamer, (Dr.), 109
Weiler, John, 85
Weiler, John G., 85
"Well Wisher", 12
Wert, Lyle, 146, 147
Wertz, (Mrs.) Charles, 146
Wertz, Charles, 146
West, William, 98
Western, William, 140
Wetzel, Fred, 82, 85, 141
Wetzel, Samuel J., 85
Whitlock, W. P., 151, 152
Widger, E. B., 49
Williams, (Councilman), 54, 56
Wilson, Ruth, 53
Wilson, Samuel, 53
Wink, Lottie, 80
Wolfe, G. D., 96
Wood, (Dr.), 94
Wooten, Sherman, 156
Worsdall, J., 35
Worsdall, John, 56
Wright, Samuel, 47, 49

Young, William, 85

www.ingramcontent.com/pod-product-compliance
Lightning Source LLC
Chambersburg PA
CBHW070142080526
44586CB00015B/1803